D0956914

Less Stuff

Less Stuff is a low-waste project, with the editorial
and design processes performed electronically.
The book is printed on stock certified by the
Forest Stewardship Council (FSC): the highest
standard forest certification scheme and a
member of ISEAL Alliance, the global association
for sustainability standards. The paper is cut to
size prior to printing to reduce wastage, and any
excess paper, plastic, wood and metal (such as
printing plates) produced during the printing
process is recycled. The book is also printed
using sustainable soy-based inks, which produce
less volatile organic compounds (VOCs) than
petroleum-based alternatives and make it easier
for any extra inventory to eventually be recycled.

Less Stuff

Simple zero-waste steps to a joyful and clutter-free life

Lindsay Miles

Hardie Grant

BOOKS

Contents

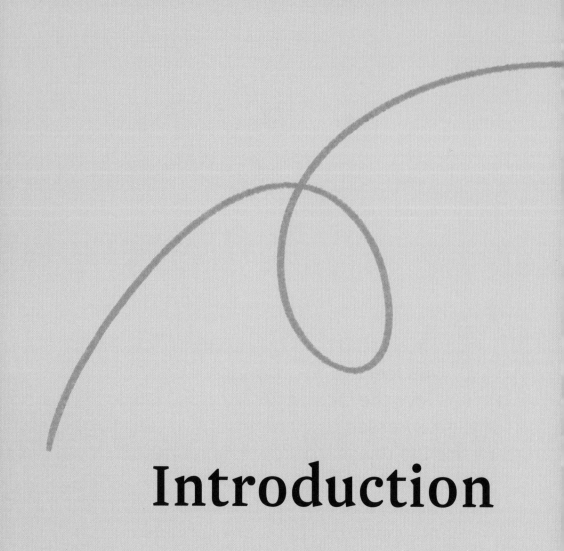

Introduction

Do you feel like you have too much stuff?
Do you love the *idea* of decluttering, getting rid
of the non-essentials and making space in your
life for the things that are truly important, but
you're not quite sure where to start? Do you worry
about waste, and hold on to things you know in
your heart you don't need because you can't bear
the thought of throwing them in the bin? Would
you like to find a way of letting go that doesn't
mean contributing to landfill, or overloading the
charity shops? Is your stuff making you feel a
little bit guilty? Do you want to let go of the
guilt once and for all?

When we think about how we love to spend our time, we don't think about sorting, or cleaning, or tidying. We want to spend less time doing the boring stuff, and more time on the things that matter. Things like catching up with friends and family, connecting with others and pursuing our dreams. Mess and clutter stand in the way of our productivity, stress us out and keep us stuck. Our stuff stands in the way of the lives we dream about.

Decluttering does not come naturally to me. I have more hoarding tendencies than minimalist tendencies – or at least, I did. Yet over time, I've learned to let go of things that I don't need. I've created space and freed up time. I've recognised that my possessions were holding me back, and making me feel anxious and guilty. I've found freedom from the pursuit of more, and, as a result of letting go of things that had a hold on me, I'm happier than I've ever been. I've found my 'enough'. Want to know how I got from there to here? Let me tell you my story.

Decluttering is a skill, and, like so many skills, it comes down to practice. I had neither at the start of my journey. When I think about why I was hoarding stuff in the first place, there were a couple of reasons. One was that I cared about waste; I wasn't going to sling perfectly useful items in the bin, and I hadn't actually stopped to think about the alternatives. I was the person keeping things *just in case*. However, there was more to it than that. I'd never needed to declutter. I'd never learned to let things go. Somehow I'd let the fact that stuff was inherently useful blur the real question: Was it useful to *me*?

As a kid, my bedroom was spacious, which meant there was plenty of room for stuff. I loved to collect things. There was never any need to get rid of anything, nor any inclination to do so. As I grew too old for toys and games, they were simply stored in the attic for 'later'. I was never encouraged to part with my things, and so I didn't.

When I left school and moved across the country to study, later travelling and then renting, my excess stuff was stored at my parents' place. I never had to deal with these things, to ask myself if I really needed them. By storing them, I put thinking about them aside.

Every Christmas and birthday, I'd accumulate more stuff. When I started working and began to earn my own money, I'd buy things that I liked, or needed, or wanted to purchase to cheer myself up. The amount of stuff I owned grew. I began to notice that the things I was receiving as gifts weren't things that I needed. They were 'better' versions of things that I already had – with which there was nothing wrong – or they were similar to things that

I already had. Another handbag, another necklace, another pair of shoes. I justified keeping this stuff by telling myself that even if it wasn't useful now, it could be in the future. I'd confuse liking something with a reason to buy it, or to keep it. I had a wardrobe full of clothes I didn't wear, which made me feel guilty every time I looked at them. Yet I always felt like I had nothing to wear, which would spur me to buy even more... but this only led to more guilt. Embracing second-hand shopping made things worse: there were so many bargains that I seemed to accumulate more than ever before.

When I moved to Australia from the UK, you'd assume I'd have got rid of everything. I did get rid of the really big stuff: most of the furniture I owned, and stuff that couldn't be stored at my parents' house. But – you guessed it – the stuff that *could* be taken to my folks' was packed into boxes and stored. Just in case.

In Australia, starting afresh, I was determined not to acquire unnecessary stuff. I deliberately chose a small flat. Yet as the months passed, my home filled up with stuff I needed, along with stuff I thought I needed, and stuff I simply liked the look of. I started to notice my home was feeling squishy. Should I move to a bigger place? It was a turning point. I didn't want to pay more rent just to store a bunch of things I rarely used. I didn't need more storage.

I needed *less stuff*. That was when my journey really began.

Bear in mind – I was somebody who had never really tried to declutter before. Plus, I was fixated on this idea of not wasting stuff. It was a recipe for disaster. The first time I decided to declutter, it *was* a complete disaster. I dedicated a long weekend to the process. For three days, I mostly sat in a chair dreaming of how I wanted my space to be decluttered already, yet I was very reluctant to find anything to get rid of. I thought I was willing, but when it came down to it, I needed it all! At the end of the long weekend, I had decluttered a single box of stuff.

Despite this failure, I was determined to keep going. I could see the benefits that came with a life with less stuff, and that's what kept me motivated to continue trying. I came across the concept of minimalism, the practice of intentionally living with less and letting go of the excess. Some of the ideas minimalists were writing about struck a chord with me. But while they were big on the *why*, they were less clear on the *how*. I was sold on the benefits, and the 'after' pictures were great, but how had these minimalists gotten there? What were the secrets?

I was frustrated that other people seemed to find decluttering and letting go so easy, when I found it so hard. I put it down to the fact that I cared about waste, when they perhaps did not. Without a method or a template to follow, I started trying things my own way: setting myself challenges, trying different things, or the same thing over and over. I started to notice patterns and to understand why I was resisting.

Then I had an epiphany, a realisation that decluttering and caring about waste actually go hand in hand. Decluttering doesn't have to be about wasting stuff. It's about identifying stuff that we own that is going to waste (because we don't use it, or don't like it, or don't need it) and finding a better place for it: a place where it will actually be used. Decluttering does not have to mean landfill. We can find new homes for our things, or places where the resources can be used again. Actually, it's an important part of the process. Decluttering can be the opposite of waste.

Once I changed my perspective, I began to make real progress. The start may have been shaky and slow, but once I really understood what I was resisting, and allowed myself time, the results came much more quickly. I learned to turn the guilt around. Getting rid of things I didn't use or need wasn't a reason to feel guilty: keeping them was! Even decluttering my wardrobe, which I'd been struggling with (despite hearing that it's the easiest place to tackle), came within my grasp.

As I let more go, my idea of 'enough' began to shift. I'd declutter down to what I considered the essentials, then realise that there were still more things to let go of. Today I'm happy that I'm close to my enough, but I'm not perfect, and I'm still experimenting with less.

I want to be comfortable, and not take it to extremes. But I'm no longer exasperated with stuff, or endless piles of clutter. I no longer have a full wardrobe but nothing to wear. I don't know how many items I own, and I'm not interested in counting, but I know where everything is (more or less), and what everything is. There are no mystery boxes or random drawers or ominous cupboards.

If I see something pretty in a shop, I acknowledge that I like it, but don't feel the urge to buy it. If other people try to offload their unwanted things on me, I politely decline. Decluttering my own stuff is hard enough without taking on other people's guilt.

I've redefined how I think of waste, too. If I have things I no longer need, I can let go of them responsibly. I may not need them, but if they still have life in them, they can be passed on to someone who can make use of them. It is more wasteful to keep things I don't need than it is to let them be used to their full potential.

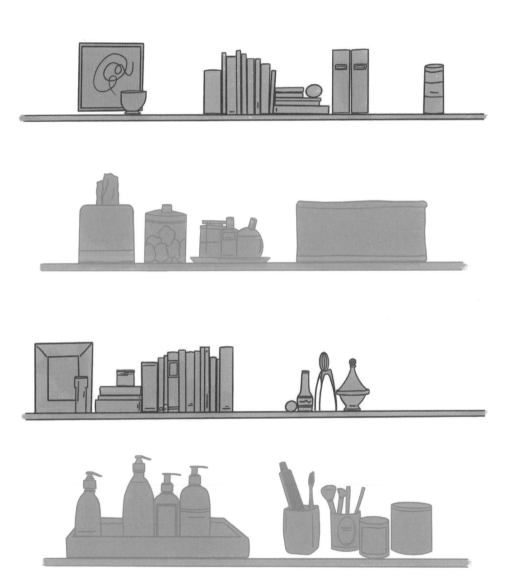

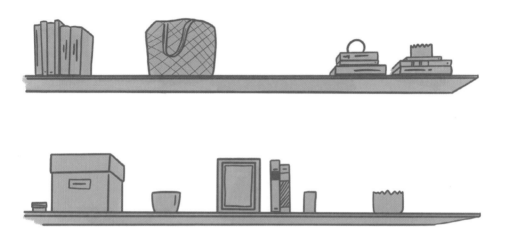

It took me three years to get here. Three long years! I would have arrived a whole lot sooner if some of the insights I had along the way had revealed themselves earlier; the benefits of hindsight and experience would have been invaluable. As a way to document the lessons I learned and help others struggling with the same things as me, I started my blog, Treading My Own Path, in 2013. Writing about living with less stuff and less waste (and how I've turned zero-waste and minimalist ideals into actionable solutions), I've been able to share my journey and help thousands of readers find their 'enough', make peace with their possessions and let go of the unnecessary – without sending it all to landfill.

Decluttering doesn't have to be a never-ending process. It can be challenging, and it can take time, but there is an end, and you can get there if you take the right approach. I hope that sharing my experiences will help to make your decluttering journey a speedier and more productive one than mine. I hope you can learn from my mistakes, and benefit from the strategies I'm sharing. If I can do it, I know that you can do it too.

This book is a guide for those of us who don't find decluttering easy, but who can see that letting go of excess stuff is necessary if we are to create more space and meaning in our lives. It is a guide for those of us who want to declutter, but who also care about where things end up when we let them go. We want to make the most of what we have, figure out what we need and responsibly let go of the rest.

Less Stuff offers structure, motivation and support to guide you as you decide what to let go, how to let go of it, and how to break the cycle.

○ We'll talk about the why, and the bigger picture.

○ We'll discuss barriers and the obstacles that you may come across, with ideas on how to overcome them.

○ We'll delve into the how. So many guides seem to skip straight from the 'before' to the 'after', with no mention of 'how'! *Less Stuff* will take you through your home step by step, and help you choose which things to let go.

○ We'll also talk about how to let go of your things responsibly. If you care about waste, you'll find this section particularly important.

○ We'll discuss what's next: techniques for keeping clutter at bay and tips for making this a one-time journey. Because there's no fun in doing it all again, is there?

My aim is to show you that a life with less stuff is achievable, possible and within your grasp ... and give you the tools to make it happen. I know decluttering can be hard. I've been there. I've experienced the struggles and the challenges and the frustration; I've also experienced the wins and the successes and the triumphs, and I know that a life with less is possible. I've seen the benefits of decluttering first-hand, and I want to help you see them too. Let's do this together.

The Bigger Picture

01

Zero Waste vs Minimalism

Zero waste and minimalism sound like opposites. Surely one is about hanging on to stuff and throwing nothing away, and the other is about discarding everything? Despite their seemingly different ideals, they actually have the same philosophy: wasting less. It's just that they approach it from different angles.

What is zero waste?

Imagine if there was no need for landfill. What if the things we purchased were made well, built to last and designed in such a way that they could be readily repaired, easily repurposed or their materials simply recovered to make new products? Rather than burying the things we no longer need in a hole in the ground for all eternity (or incinerating them into ash and smoke), these items, or the materials they are made from, could become resources for others to use for years to come.

That is the philosophy behind zero waste. If we look at how things work in nature, there is no waste. Nature cycles and recycles everything: air, water, nutrients. Humans are the only species known to create waste.

And what a lot of waste we create! The reality is that many of the things we purchase are not made to last a lifetime, and they aren't easy to repair if and when they do break. When items are made of mixed materials (such as wood, different types of plastic and different metals) it is not easy to recycle them. It is hard to know what to do with these things other than toss them in the bin.

This isn't an accident on the part of manufacturers. Many manufacturers deliberately design products to break or wear out. There is even a term for it: planned obsolescence, which means 'designed for the dump'.

Manufacturers do this to keep us buying their products. There's a balance they need to find – if things break too easily, we might not go back to their product. If an item lasts forever, they won't be able to sell us a new one. Products need to last just long enough for us to trust the manufacturer enough to buy a replacement, but expire quickly enough that they can sell us a new product as soon as possible. The old item? That likely ends up in landfill.

Surely things can be done differently? That is where zero waste comes in.

Zero waste is both an industrial design term and a lifestyle philosophy. The term was first coined in the 1970s by a chemist called Dr Paul Palmer, who noticed that companies in Silicon Valley were discarding chemicals that were still perfectly usable. He set up a company (Zero Waste Systems Inc.) to find uses for and resell all of the chemicals that were being discarded.

Palmer recognised that the best way to avoid waste is for everything to be reused indefinitely, and this can only be achieved if reuse is designed into products, rather than only being considered once a product reaches the end of its useful life. He saw zero waste as a design principle.

Most of us are not product designers. We are people who buy things in good faith, and only realise that these things are not durable or fixable or recyclable once they break or wear out, and we are faced with putting them in the bin. But we still have the power to make a difference through our everyday choices and the purchases we make. This is what the zero-waste lifestyle is all about: how individuals can reduce the rubbish they create at home.

The zero-waste lifestyle movement started in 2008, when Bea Johnson began her blog, Zero Waste Home, detailing how her family avoided throwing anything in their bin. Instead, they focused on refusing things they did not need, reducing and reusing – with recycling as the last resort. Today there are thousands of people doing what they can to limit what they put in the bin.

Designing products that can be reused in perpetuity and not throwing anything in the bin might sound fantastic, but is it realistic? Well, it is true that zero waste in its purest form doesn't actually exist. Not yet. That's why zero waste is often described as a set of guiding principles, a goal, or a philosophy. We might not be able to achieve perfection, but we can still do what we can with what we have. We can make better choices, not just with our purchases in the future, but also with how we dispose of the things that we own now.

Sending nothing to landfill doesn't mean simply storing stuff that's broken, irreparable and useless in our homes instead of putting it in the rubbish bin; it doesn't mean making our living spaces a pseudo-landfill. It's about choosing to use resources wisely.

Zero-waste living means:

○ refusing products and packaging that are single-use or poorly made, flimsy and non-repairable

○ reducing our consumption to only what is necessary ('necessary' may differ from person to person – it's a personal choice, of course, and we all have different needs – but it comes down to mindful consumption, not buying stuff simply because it was on sale at a bargain price/looked appealing in the advert/the next-door neighbour has one)

○ reusing items we already have, and choosing reusables over single-use items

○ repairing items when they break, rather than simply chucking them out in favour of new ones (which is why choosing well-made and easy-to-repair products is important), or repurposing them so that they can continue to be useful

- ○ recycling only what cannot be reused, repaired or repurposed

- ○ rotting, or composting, the scraps that cannot be dealt with any other way.

The zero-waste lifestyle follows these and as a result next to nothing is sent to landfill.

What is minimalism?

In a world that teaches us that accumulating stuff is good, that happiness can be found through shopping and that more is better, minimalism is a deliberate decision to slow down, to look at our possessions and our lifestyles. It's about letting go of the excess, getting rid of the non-essential and focusing on what brings joy and creates meaning in our lives – experiences, connections and people. The things that make us truly happy are not things at all.

Minimalism is about finding freedom from the pursuit of more, and contentment with what we already have ... or maybe even a little bit less.

Our material-obsessed lifestyle is relatively new. Many of our grandparents grew up during war and economic depression. They often didn't have the material comforts we take for granted today or even their basic needs met. The baby-boomer generation of the 1950s were the first to be able to buy everything they needed. Having seen the struggles their parents went through, it's easy to understand why the baby boomers saw possessions as a means to happiness. Up to a point, of course, this is true. But they met their basic needs ... and kept on going, accumulating more and more. Maybe it's the hunter-gatherer instinct that we used to our advantage for thousands of years – we just haven't learned how to use the 'off' switch.

The truth is, this explosion of consumerism hasn't resulted in a corresponding growth in happiness. In fact, happiness is thought to have peaked in the 1960s. Instead, we're stressed, we're time-poor and we're unhappy ... and buying our way out of it hasn't worked. Our stuff has begun to own us. Plus we're using up resources at an alarming rate.

Minimalism is not about wasting stuff, and it is definitely not about chucking stuff in the bin to make space to acquire new stuff. It's not about only owning one hundred items, or never spending any money. It is not about living in a modern home with sleek designer furniture, or living in a shack in the wilderness. Maybe for some minimalists these lifestyle choices do apply, but for many more none of these apply. It is not about following 'rules' (except the ones we make ourselves) or pursuing the least amount of things.

Minimalism is simply a journey to 'enough', to discovering the right amount of things for us, and letting go of the excess. It is about spending less money on stuff so there's less debt and more freedom. It's about spending less time cleaning and tidying and organising (and shopping!) so there's more time for the stuff that's really important – spending time with friends and family, hobbies, helping others and getting involved with our local community.

Can you be a zero-waste minimalist?

Zero waste and minimalism: are they really that different? I don't think so. At the heart of both is the idea of intentional living. Realising what we truly need, making do and choosing well. Being mindful, making conscious choices and living life with purpose. Two sides of the same coin. Of course, you can aspire to one lifestyle but not the other. There are plenty of people passionate about zero waste who are not minimalists, and many minimalists who do not live a zero-waste lifestyle.

You can be zero waste, you can be minimalist, you can be both... and you can be neither. When it comes to labels, some of us love them, and some of us don't. If you're a fan of moderation and these labels just seem too extreme for you, don't use them. This isn't about striving for perfection. It's about doing the best we can. You can know you have too much stuff and want to have less, without wanting to call yourself a minimalist. You can be keen to recycle more, and send less to landfill, without wanting to do away with your rubbish bin entirely and be zero waste.

We all have our own version of enough. Find yours. It doesn't matter what anybody else's looks like, nor what they call it. This is about you, your stuff, your relationship to your stuff, and how you're going to change that for the better.

02

Why Decluttering Can Be Good for the Planet

Decluttering (when done right) is actually good for the planet. Decluttering is *not* good for the planet if everything that is being decluttered ends up at the nearest landfill site, regardless of its condition and usability.

Decluttering is good when we try our best to find new homes for the things we no longer need, repurpose and repair what we can, and recycle the rest. It's good for the planet because it frees up existing resources and reduces the demand for the extraction of raw materials and the manufacture of new products.

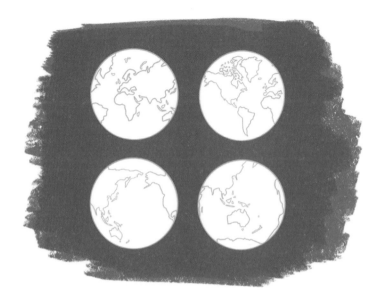

Humans use a lot of resources. We use more resources than we have, or rather we are using them faster than they can be renewed. The Global Footprint Network calculates Earth Overshoot Day each year to mark the date when our demand for ecological resources and services exceeds what Earth can regenerate in that year. They also calculate what date the world would run out of resources if everybody lived like the people of a given country. In 2018, Overshoot Day was 15 March in the US, 31 March in Australia and 8 May in the UK.

What this means is that if everyone in the world lived in the same way as Americans or Australians do, we'd need four planets to sustain us.

The reality, of course, is that we only have one. The good news is, decluttering is an opportunity to put resources that aren't being used back into society, and make them available for other people to use.

No one declutters items that they love, need and use all the time. The things that we declutter are the things we no longer need, never use and don't like. These things serve no real purpose in our homes; they simply sit there taking up space and gathering dust. At the same time, someone in the world will be looking for exactly that item.

They say one person's trash is another's treasure, and it is truer than you think.

By putting these products back into circulation, we allow others to give them a new home and extend their life. Making second-hand and preloved items available helps reduce the purchase of new products. Less demand for new products means fewer are made.

Even when things are broken or damaged, there is often the opportunity to repair or repurpose them, use them for parts, or recycle them. Recycling uses energy, but it uses a lot less energy than creating brand-new resources from raw materials.

There will be things that we need to declutter that are useless – damaged beyond repair, hazardous to our health, dangerous or simply not valuable enough to be worth recycling. These things have reached the end of their useful life: they are waste already. Their journey to landfill is inevitable, and decluttering them is no worse than letting them languish in the shed. When we let these things go, we have an opportunity to learn from our mistakes and make better choices next time round.

Mindful consumption starts with mindful decluttering

The benefits of decluttering are talked about often: less clutter, less stress, less time spent tidying; more space in our homes, more time to do the things we love. Less burden, more freedom.

That is the end result we want. However, in our enthusiasm to get to the end and be 'finished' as soon as possible, we can forget that the journey is just as important as the destination. In many ways the journey is more important. This is where the lessons are learned.

It's easy to think that once we have decluttered, then things will be different. We'll embrace new habits and make better choices. We will be more mindful when we make purchases. We will think more carefully before bringing stuff into our homes. However, if we don't take the time to consider why we made the purchases originally and why we are getting rid of them now, we aren't setting ourselves up for the best chance of success in the future.

We all have a legacy of purchases that, with the benefit of hindsight, we wouldn't have made. However tempting it might be to toss the unwanted stuff aside as quickly as possible and start over with a clean slate, there is another way: one that is far more rewarding. We can own our bad choices, and find good solutions for the things we no longer need. We stand a much better chance of changing our habits if we take our time to let things go, and learn from the process.

Part of this is considering how best we can pass on items that we no longer like, need or want. Often, we don't give any thought to what will happen to the purchases we make until they break or we realise we don't need them any more. It is only then that we start to ask the questions:

○ What do I do with it now?

○ Is it repairable?

○ Is it recyclable?

○ Would someone else be able to use it?

If we want to ensure that our future purchases are things that are made to last and that we will use, we need to be asking these questions before we buy things. We want to make considered purchases. That is mindful consumption. And the more we learn from mindfully letting go of our previous mistakes – things that were difficult to donate, impossible to fix and designed for the dump – the easier it is to make better choices next time.

Need not, waste not

There are plenty of reasons why we find it so hard to let go of our stuff. We'll explore the emotional reasons in the next section, but first let's consider a very practical concern for many of us. We feel that

getting rid of stuff is a waste of resources. If we care about the impact we're having on the planet, and worry about the embedded energy of the stuff we own (embedded energy is the energy it took to manufacture and transport the product in the first place), then being concerned about the waste can mean real reluctance to let go of items.

The reality is, there is more than one way to waste stuff, and 'Do I need it?' is a much better first question than 'Is getting rid of it a waste?' If we don't need an item, we can explore how to let go of it in a way that isn't creating waste. Keeping stuff we don't need is a waste, not the other way round. If, in an attempt to avoid waste, we are keeping items we never use, we are simply turning our homes into personal landfills. That is not a solution. Really, how is keeping something in a cupboard and never using it any different to simply throwing it away?

Of course, throwing something in the bin is a complete waste of resources, but as we've talked about already, decluttering doesn't have to mean sending everything to landfill. There is a difference between things we don't use but that still have plenty of life left in them, and broken, useless items. For some of us, getting rid of broken items is actually more difficult than finding new homes for the good stuff. That's because giving items we no longer require to people who will use them or

repurpose them can alleviate some of the guilt that comes from wasting resources. When it comes to broken stuff that really has no use, no value and no potential for reuse, the only option is landfill, and landfill can feel like a failure.

If something truly has no use, no value and no reuse potential, keeping it in our home is simply delaying the inevitable. Some things are designed for the dump, and as much as we wish things were different, that is the reality. If an item isn't being used, it is going to waste, regardless of whether it is in our home or the local landfill site. Let it go, and resolve to make better choices in future.

The 'waste' argument is no excuse to keep useful items that you don't actually use. If you're genuinely concerned about waste, there are plenty of ways to connect things you don't need with people who will use them (we'll cover this later). If you regret having spent money on brand-new items you've never used, the advantage is that you should be able to sell them for a reasonable price. Even worn and used items often have a second-hand market, so there's an opportunity to recoup some of the money you spent, which can help soften the blow. However, financial recompense isn't everything.

Being able to gift something to someone in genuine need of it is another, very rewarding option. How can we feel guilty about letting something go when we see the joy of others in receiving it?

Whichever way we decide to do it, finding people who will use our stuff is the best use of resources and the best way to let go of guilt. Don't let your hang-ups about previous purchases cloud or influence the real decision: whether you need something or not.

Remember, if you don't need it and don't use it, it is already going to waste.

On the fence about something? Ask these questions.

Do I need it now?

Have I used it in the last six months?

Can I imagine a time in the next six months when I might need it?

How realistic is it that I will need it again?

Is there something I already own that I could use/make do with instead?

Would I be able to borrow something similar from someone I know?

Would I be able to hire it rather than buying a replacement?

Would I be able to find it (or something similar) in the charity shop, or second-hand?

Do I have the budget to purchase a replacement?

How quickly would I be able to find a replacement?

How important would it be to be able to find a replacement quickly?

Would there be any physical or practical restrictions on getting a replacement easily?

03

Broadening Your Horizons

Once we identify things we no longer need and decide to declutter them, it can be all too tempting to charge down to the charity shop with most of them and send the rest off with the nearest rubbish truck in our haste to be finished. But we can still work quickly without limiting our thinking to just two options – and do better by the environment and by others in the process. This is our opportunity to let someone else make good use of our stuff, save resources, help those less fortunate and learn a lot about ourselves and our habits along the way. So what are the options for our unwanted things?

Reuse

The first and best result for our stuff is for it to be reused. This means somebody taking it and using it again without needing to modify it in any way. Ideally an item can be reused in exactly the way it was designed for: clothes worn again as clothes rather than being chopped up into rags, for example. Donating things to community groups and organisations that need them or can pass them on to people in need ensures their reuse, as does donating things to charity shops where they can be resold. Selling items to people who want what we have, whether online or in person (say via a garage sale), is another example of reuse.

Of course, there is never an absolute guarantee that something will be reused in the way intended, but we can make best guesses and do our part.

Repurpose

The next best use is for an item to be repurposed. This means the item will be reused, but will be modified in some way or used for a different purpose to the one intended. An old bike wheel being used in an artwork or a teacup being used as a plant pot are examples of repurposing.

Community gardens will often repurpose materials to make garden beds, signage and other structures; schools, playgroups and arts and crafts organisations might use materials for projects; and there are plenty of crafty individuals making useful products by repurposing materials.

Repair

Sometimes items need to be repaired before they can be reused. Whether that means a button stitched back on, a part or component replaced or a fresh coat of paint applied, repairing something can bring an item back to life and extend its usefulness for years. It is far easier to donate and sell products that are in working order than it is a broken item. The options are to fix things ourselves or find someone that can fix them for us (a friend who knows how to sew, for example, or a cobbler who can re-heel a pair of shoes for a small fee).

Broken items given to a charity shop will most likely end up in landfill. Donating (or even selling) broken items is not impossible though – the task is to find someone willing and eager to fix it. Some people love to mend things or tinker with them and will be eager to take them off our hands – and if the fixed product will have a value, they might even pay for the privilege.

Recycle

When items cannot be reused, repurposed or repaired, the next best option is to recycle. Recycling processes materials so that they can be reused, and then reforms these materials into new products. Metals might be melted down, papers pulped and plastics shredded into pellets that can be remoulded. It takes a lot of energy to collect, treat and process materials, which is why it is preferable to reuse or repurpose an item where possible. However, recycling still keeps resources out of landfill, conserves energy, reduces demand for new material extraction and is a better option than throwing things away.

Recycling isn't limited to our day-to-day household waste such as packaging. Many things can be recycled: textiles, tyres, paint, batteries, metals, timber, electronics. They might not go in the kerbside collection but recycling services for these items exist, and we can make use of them to give the materials we no longer require a new lease of life.

Landfill

The last resort is sending our stuff to landfill. We might have items for which there is no other option but this. However, landfill should be the solution for the minority of the things we declutter, not the majority. There are so many other options to consider first. When we do have to landfill our old items, we can use it as a learning experience. We can consider why these things ended up in landfill in the first place, and use these lessons to inform our future purchasing decisions so we choose better next time.

There is a whole spectrum of choices and opportunities for our stuff. As we begin to identify items we no longer need, keep in mind these ideas and ask the question: What would really be the best outcome for these things?

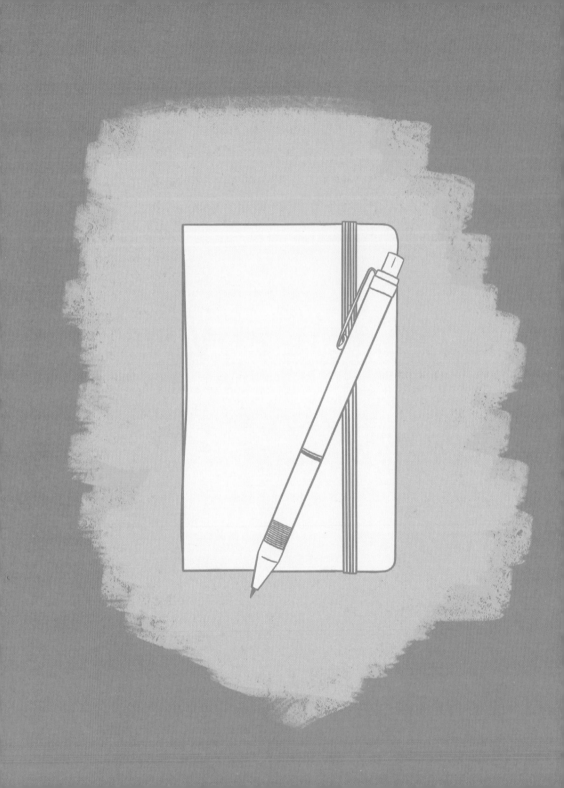

Before We Begin

Getting Clear
on Values

04

When it comes to making changes to our lives, it can be tempting to just dive right in and 'do stuff'. However, to give ourselves the best chance of success there's a little mental preparation we can embrace before we leap into action: thinking about why we want to make those changes.

Our values are like our guiding force. They are often subconscious and are shaped by our life experiences, our education, cultural and societal norms, and the money we have at our disposal. These values determine the goals we set, the attitudes we have and the behaviour we display.

Advertisements tap in to what we value, and then activate these values to persuade us to buy products. They show us happy, healthy people who have loving families and friends and beautiful, well-behaved children – people who live in stylish (and clutter-free) homes, have stress-free lives and spend time outdoors. In this way the advertiser implies that their product will make our lives like this too – we can resolve our insecurities through shopping. We buy the product, but the reality doesn't match. Deep down we know that new crockery or better shampoo won't make us happier, more loved or less stressed, yet we are bombarded with these ideas all the time, and it is easy to succumb to them. Once the thrill of the purchase has faded, however, nothing has changed. Our insecurities and worries remain.

There is another way. Rather than relying on adverts to tell us what's best for us, and what will make us happy, we can get clear on our values and make conscious choices based on what we know is important to us. You might have an idea that you want to declutter, or to simplify, but perhaps you haven't yet considered your why. Now is the time to delve deeper and explore what this really means for you.

Getting clear on what we're doing and exactly why we are doing it is the first step towards making change that lasts. At the beginning of trying anything new we can be all hyped up, full of excitement and raring to go, but as soon as we hit a stumbling block, or come up against a challenge that's a little harder than we expected, it's easy to fall off the wagon. We need to know what we're trying to achieve, to know in our heart that it is the right thing to do and to know why we're doing it. That will give us the motivation to get back up, dust ourselves off and try again.

What is it that you really value?

Let's dive into the deep stuff. What do you love to do, and how do you want to spend your time? We get more joy from life when we spend our free time doing what we love and being more present with people we love. If you sometimes spend your free time doing one thing while your head is somewhere else, or you feel overwhelmed with chores and tasks and to-do lists, think about how decluttering and simplifying might give you the space you need.

Ask yourself the following questions – and be honest.

Where are my favourite places?

What are my most treasured childhood memories?

Who are the people I most enjoy spending time with?

What activities do I find personally fulfilling and rewarding?

What things would I love to do more of?

What am I doing when I'm happiest?

How could less stuff and less clutter help me be more present?

How would I feel with less stuff and less clutter?

Our spare time is precious. The less we have, the more we need to be sure we are using it to do the things we value the most.

How do I currently spend my time: days, evenings and weekends?

How does this divide up over the course of the week?

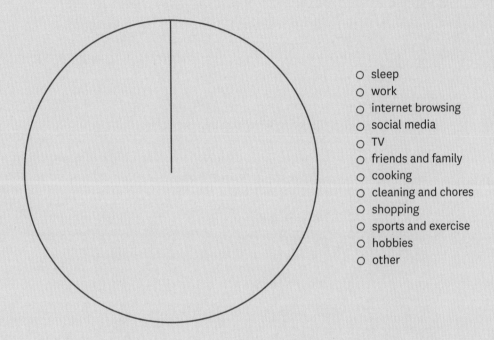

- ○ sleep
- ○ work
- ○ internet browsing
- ○ social media
- ○ TV
- ○ friends and family
- ○ cooking
- ○ cleaning and chores
- ○ shopping
- ○ sports and exercise
- ○ hobbies
- ○ other

How many hours do I spend doing the things that I love with people I love?

How many hours do I spend doing things I don't particularly enjoy?

What do I spend too much time on? What do I spend too little time on?

How could less stuff and less clutter help me find more time for the important things?

05

Overcoming the Scarcity Mindset

Simply put, a scarcity mindset is the belief that there will never be 'enough'. When it comes to decluttering, holding on to stuff can be the result of a scarcity mindset. We might realise that we have too much stuff, but we don't want to reach the point of having too *little* stuff.

How do we know what 'enough' actually is? The truth is, we don't – not until we start letting go of what we no longer need. This is how we find out how much (or how little) we really do need.

That said, no one wants to declutter things that they later realise they did have a use for after all. The idea of decluttering everything and just buying it back again if we change our mind doesn't sit well with anyone on a budget. It's also a waste of time to get rid of things only to have to track them down again later. It's a balance.

The scarcity mindset and the fear we feel when we let go of things that we might actually need later limits how much we will declutter. The question is whether the fear is justified in some way, or an excuse to hold on to something. Overcoming the scarcity mindset isn't about 'feeling the fear and doing it anyway' – in some cases the fear of decluttering an item may be entirely logical. When we declutter we simply need to be practical and realistic about our own situation. What 'enough' looks like for each of us will be different.

We need to ask the question: Realistically, what would happen if I were to let go of something and then realised I needed it later on?

The answer to this will depend on two sets of considerations.

The first relates to the item: what it is, what consequences there would be to needing the item and being without it, how easy it would be to find an alternative and how affordable a replacement would be.

The second relates to our personal situation: the place we live, our access to transport, our budget for getting a replacement and how practical it would be for us to physically get the replacement.

A set of wine glasses is likely easier to replace quickly than a specialist textbook; a customised piece of furniture that fits a difficult space will cost more to replace than a wooden chopping board. Living rurally might mean less access to shops and less ability to find a replacement; living in an urban area without a car might mean restrictions on sourcing large items that require a vehicle to transport.

There are three factors to consider when deciding whether to let go of an item we are worried that we might need again:

○ time

○ distance

○ money.

Ask yourself: How quickly would I be able to find a replacement, how far am I willing to travel for a replacement and how much money am I willing to spend? Deciding on rules that work for our situation can help make these decisions a little more rational and logical. It might be that all three factors are important, or it might be that there is only one limiting factor. How long it takes to find a replacement might not be important so long as it costs less than $20. Or perhaps the item needs to be replaceable within twenty minutes, and the cost needs to be under $100. Think about what is realistic for your time, your living situation and your budget, and refer back to this when you feel a little stuck.

If reducing waste is important to you then a fourth factor might be more relevant than the other three: Can I replace it without buying it new? Maybe time, distance and money don't matter so long as a replacement can be found second-hand.

In truth, the majority of things that you decide you don't need, you won't need. Having a back-up policy can help overcome those niggling doubts when deciding whether or not to let things go.

Storage solutions are not the solution

As tempting as it can be to buy shelving units, storage boxes, folders and binders, new labels, coloured pens – whatever it is that you have your eye on to help get your stuff 'in order' – don't make that purchase! Decluttering is about letting go of the unnecessary stuff, not hiding it or disguising it.

Buying stuff is easy. Decluttering stuff is harder. We've got the 'buying stuff' habit nailed; we don't need any more practice at that. The 'letting go of stuff' habit – that's the one we need to work on. The need to feel like we are making progress can be met with the act of buying stuff. Alas, it is the opposite of progress. If decluttering is something you struggle with, and you know you have a hard time letting things go, why would you consider buying more stuff as a solution?

Feeling like we are making progress is not the same as making progress. We can't buy our way to less stuff. We can't organise our way to less stuff. The only way we will make progress with decluttering is by actually letting stuff go. More storage is not the answer to too much stuff. Less stuff is the answer to too much stuff.

06

It's a Marathon, Not a Sprint

If you don't have much stuff to start with, you're ruthless in your approach, completely determined, keen to put the rest of your life on hold as you tackle this challenge, and you're happy to take action fast with the things you no longer need, you'll be able to progress fairly quickly. If you have a lot of stuff to work through and prefer a more considered approach, taking the time to find the absolute best new homes for your unwanted items, the journey will take a lot longer.

Whichever path you end up taking, do not underestimate the time you will need. Decluttering your home of everything you no longer love or need is not a process that you will complete in a single afternoon.

Keeping spaces clutter-free is not a case of tidying the whole house and thinking, 'Right, I'm never letting it get messy again!' (Yes, that was me. I have no idea what made me think that I could go from messy person to tidy person following one weekend of cleaning.) It's not a job that you'll finish in a week or two, either. As a minimum, you'll likely need to allow yourself six months to tackle everything. If you're just starting out on your journey, it's probable that you will need a lot longer.

This is possibly not what you want to hear. We live in an age where everything moves so fast, and we're used to quick fixes and corner-cutting life hacks and instant results. We can visualise the end result already, and we want to get there as quickly as possible. It's not enough to just know the goal. We have to do the work.

When we have all these doubts and emotions and worries intertwined with all of our stuff, it's not easy to let go – at least not at the start. When I first started out, I genuinely thought I could declutter my entire apartment in a (long) weekend. I set myself a goal to find one hundred things.

I managed less than eighty – in three days! The whole experience was a shock to me, and extremely disheartening. Several things held me back: I wasn't clear on my why, or what the wider benefits would be. I didn't understand the process of change, and I didn't expect to feel so much internal resistance. There were times when I found it all too overwhelming, and had to step back. I had to adjust to the changes I made before going on.

What I did learn was that the journey is just as important as the destination. It is the journey that teaches us the lessons we need to learn. After all, decluttering should be the end, not the means. There is no point in letting go of everything we no longer need, and making space in our homes and our lives simply to go and refill that space with another bunch of new things we don't really need. If you notice yourself feeling despondent about your 'lack of progress', remember that the process is the important part and relish the fact that you're taking time to do things properly – it will mean better, lasting results in the end. The more you let go, the easier it gets.

I know that this sounds counterintuitive (surely it's easier at the start when there's all the stuff you know you don't want?) but it's true. The more you let go, the more you loosen your grip on your possessions – the more you learn to notice the resistance you're feeling and let it pass. The more you get rid of, the more you realise that there are no terrible repercussions or nightmares, and it's easier than you thought.

Let go of your expectations. Know that it will take as long as it needs to. What you want to happen and how it unfolds will likely be different, and there's nothing wrong with that. Don't put extra pressure on yourself, and don't be disheartened if you don't get instant results.

If it all gets too much or it's making you stress ... then just ... slow ... down. Or stop, if you need to. Take a break. If you're feeling resistance, that's understandable. We tie a lot of our hopes and dreams and wants and fears into our possessions, and when we let go of our possessions we have to deal with these feelings too. That can be hard. It's okay to have bad days. Wait until you're ready, and get back on the bandwagon. Don't feel guilty if you can't get rid of something despite knowing you don't really need it. You can come back to it later.

Everything you do is a step in the right direction, and things get easier over time. Think of each action as an opportunity to become more conscious about the choices you make, and to experiment with your 'enough'. It's an opportunity to learn, to discover your limits and to grow. It's your chance to make space in your life for the things you truly value. You haven't failed until you stop trying.

Remember, if it was easy you'd already have done it.

Changing habits

Change isn't always easy: it takes patience and resilience. Of course it is possible, but don't underestimate the process. You might be trying to change habits that you've been committed to for years, possibly even decades. Rewiring those habits is unlikely to happen overnight. You have to do things consciously until they become unconscious. Think of decluttering and tidying as muscles – the more you exercise them, the stronger they get.

In their Transtheoretical (Stages of Change) Model, Prochaska and DiClemente showed how the process of change can be divided into five stages: pre-contemplation, contemplation, determination, action and maintenance.

We can enter and exit at any stage in this process, and we can cycle between two stages many times before moving on to the next one. So what do these stages mean, and what do they look like?

Pre-contemplation	We don't even realise there's a need to change. Maybe everyone else around us sees it, but we can't (or won't). There is no intention to take any action in the near future.
Contemplation	We realise that there is something that we would like to change, but we're not at the point of doing anything about it … yet. The awareness is there, and maybe we're thinking about making some changes within the next six months.
Determination	We understand that there is a need or desire to change, and we've decided to do something about it. We intend to begin within the next month. Maybe we've already taken some first steps – made some enquiries, started researching – but we haven't actually acted yet. The good news is, by reading this book, you've likely decided you'd like to make a change, so you are already at this stage!
Action	We make a change. We've altered our behaviour within the last six months and we're working towards making this new behaviour a habit. As you work through decluttering your home, you may swing between 'action' and 'determination'. This isn't going backwards; it's all part of the process.
Maintenance	We've made these changes a habit and we've been maintaining them for more than six months, and there's no intention to go back to our old ways!

Dealing with Other People (and Their Stuff)

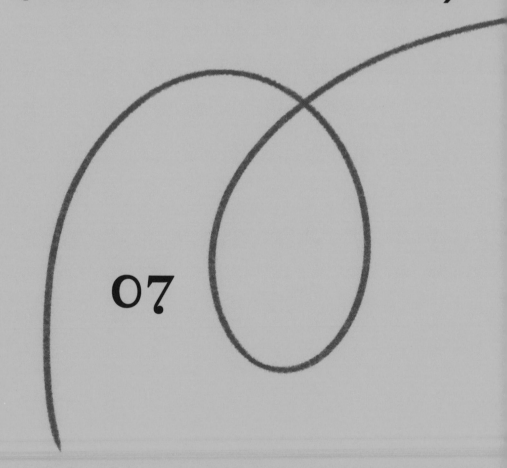

07

Now you've committed to decluttering your home, it's a good idea to tell other people. While it can be tempting to go it alone, especially if you're worried that you won't get the results you want or the support you'd like, there are a couple of good reasons for sharing what you're about to do.

First, there's nothing like declaring your intentions to the world to encourage action. Nobody wants to look like a flake, so tell everyone what you're going to do – it makes everything feel more real, and there will be far more incentive for you to do it! Not only that, but the people you tell will keep you accountable. They will ask you how it's going and, believe me, it feels far better to report back in the affirmative!

Second, if you're lucky, people will be super supportive. At the other end of the scale, they might tell you that it's a ridiculous idea and you're wasting your time (hopefully not, but families and friends can be a little outspoken sometimes). Whatever they say, remember that this is your journey. You don't need permission, and it doesn't matter what anyone else thinks. Turn any negative energy around and use it to your advantage – as an extra incentive for proving the naysayers wrong!

Don't make the mistake of treating support or enthusiasm from others as a desire to actually join in. They may think it's a great idea but not be at the stage of the journey where they are ready to take action themselves. Bear in mind too, they might be using the opportunity to encourage getting rid of your stuff, not deal with their own. Be wary of tackling your stuff together: they probably won't feel the same way as you about your childhood toys or Grandma's heirloom crockery. If they really want to join in, it will likely work better if they deal with their own stuff, and you deal with yours.

Of course, you may have a friend or family member who is genuinely just as keen as you to get started, who you know will be helpful and supportive, and whose assistance is likely to be a real asset to you. If that's the case, great! You'll be able to keep each other motivated and speed the journey along. If you know that this will work for you, embrace it.

There is one cardinal rule when it comes to decluttering – absolutely DO NOT declutter anyone else's stuff without their permission (and be careful of decluttering 'joint' stuff without asking). Yes, it can be very tempting! But it is not going to endear you to anybody. Instead, this is a sure-fire way to start fights and build resentment. Don't nag others to do it either, and don't make snide comments or 'helpful' suggestions. Even if you're asked, remember decluttering can be hard and emotion-filled, so try to keep your advice general and avoid making personal comments.

You may feel that your own stuff is just a small proportion of the general clutter in your home (and most of us do!), but that stuff of yours is where your focus has to be. This is your journey. Of course you want the other people in your life to come with you, but don't drag them along if they're digging in their heels. Show them the way, and set them a path to follow.

A word on gifts

Some people love to give gifts, and they choose to express their appreciation for others this way. We can be gracious and grateful and flattered that someone thought highly enough of us to give a gift, but if we don't like the gift, we don't need to keep it out of guilt.

Imagine it was the other way round. Would you rather a friend kept a gift they didn't like, feeling guilty that you'd wasted your money or that you'd misjudged their taste whenever they saw it, or would you rather they gave it to someone who loved it and made good use of it?

The purpose of a gift is the act of giving. That's where the meaning lies, not in the physical object that is given.

08

Coming Up
Against Resistance

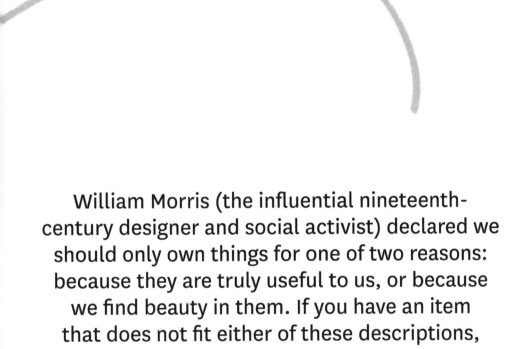

William Morris (the influential nineteenth-century designer and social activist) declared we should only own things for one of two reasons: because they are truly useful to us, or because we find beauty in them. If you have an item that does not fit either of these descriptions, but you feel you cannot let it go, then you need to consider why that is.

We resist letting go of things for a number of reasons. While these may seem quite irrational, they can have a very powerful effect on us. They are linked to emotions, fears, dreams and values – and these are heavyweight feelings to disrupt and challenge. Learning to notice them is the first step in letting go.

Remember, recognising the reason for resistance does not necessarily mean that you will be able to overcome it straightaway. The next step is acceptance … and that can take time. But you are already on the journey, and you are closer than you think.

Regret for the past

The biggest reason for resistance is guilt – or, if we think about it another way, regret for the past. We've all got stuff in our homes that we keep out of guilt. Maybe it's a gift we've been given that really isn't our taste, a dress that actually suited the model in the catalogue far more than it suits us, the jeans that haven't fitted for three years, the bargain that saved so much money but we still haven't used. We feel guilty because we wish things were different.

Feeling guilty isn't a good thing. Feeling like you've failed every time you see something (failed to like something, failed to look like someone else, failed to stop enjoying chocolate more than salad, failed to resist the temptation of the bargain) isn't healthy, and it isn't helpful. It's not a motivation to change; it's a reminder that we didn't.

Don't think of it as failing, because it isn't. There was a lesson in there to be learned. We can take the lesson on board and let the item go.

Fear of the future

Another reason that we keep stuff we don't need is 'just in case' – or fear of the future. If you have items in your home that you don't love and don't need, and you're not keeping them out of guilt, chances are you're keeping them just in case. These can be items we used to use but no longer do, items that we've been given that we've never used, or items that we plan to start using in future … when we get the time/ skills/energy to do so. The truth is, 'just in case' will probably never happen.

'Just in case' will mean different things to all of us, but owning a torch in case there's a power failure is a very different scenario to owning a watercolour set in case we ever decide to take up painting. If you know that you could replace it quickly, easily and within your budget (particularly if it is something you know you could borrow or find second-hand)

there's no need to keep something just in case. Let these items go. If you change your mind later, you can always get another. Chances are, though, you won't.

Your fantasy self

We all have a fantasy self. The 'us' that has much more time than we do, and all of the characteristics that we aspire to have. Fantasy us doesn't flop down on the sofa and start scrolling through social media after a hard day of work, oh no. Fantasy us is being incredibly productive: learning French, or polishing the ornaments, or reupholstering the antique chair we've had in the shed for years.

Our fantasy self doesn't exist. No one is perfect, and we often overcommit our time and energy to more than we can fit in to our days. We also have to be true to who we actually are, what makes us comfortable and how we like to live our lives in the day-to-day. There's a fine line between actual dreams and aspirations, and vague wants, desires and things we 'like the idea of'.

When we like an idea, but not enough to prioritise it, the items that are attached to the idea remain unused. We might think we love them (or rather, the idea attached to them) but if it is our fantasy self that has accumulated the items, we will never use them. We need to recognise our fantasy self in order to let these items go.

Sometimes we use our stuff to create an identity for ourselves, or to demonstrate to others who we are (or who we'd like them to think we are). This may be conscious or subconscious, but we choose possessions that we think send a message to others and we like what they say about us, but for what end? It's just more stuff cluttering up our homes.

O Are all those unread books sitting on the shelves because, while fantasy us loves the idea of being well read, actual us never prioritises sitting down with a good book?

O Are all the high heels in the corner of the wardrobe unworn because while fantasy us loves a pair of killer heels, actual us prefers to walk in sensible flats?

O Are the dining room cupboards piled high with crockery that is never used because, while fantasy us loves the idea of entertaining at home, the real us would much rather go out with friends to a restaurant?

We don't need belongings to show other people who we are. We are who we are regardless of what we own, and we must have the confidence to acknowledge that we are enough just as we are, without all these accessories.

The good news is, when we declutter the belongings of our fantasy self, we also declutter the expectations that come with them. We no longer feel pressured by our belongings to make changes that we know in our hearts we won't ever make.

Your inner critic

As well as a fantasy self, we all have self-doubt, and there's nothing like embarking on a new challenge or trying to learn a new habit to bring it to the surface.

If you're someone who can talk yourself out of something and accept defeat before you've even started, this reminder is for you! Maybe you've tried to declutter before, maybe several times. What happened then doesn't matter. Don't let the self-doubter in your head tell you otherwise. Those experiences all led to being here now, and strengthened your resolve to try again. Remember, all things are difficult before they are easy, and struggle makes success all the more sweet.

Allow yourself the best chance of success, and give yourself permission. That might sound fluffy, but it's all about preparing yourself mentally for whatever might come your way. Knowing in advance that it might not all go according to plan, but pushing on regardless. Letting resistance come up, but rather than letting it dictate your behaviour, simply acknowledging that it is there.

Give yourself permission to:

O commit 100 per cent to giving this your best shot to let go of anything that you no longer need

O focus on the present, without regretting the past or worrying unnecessarily about the future

O observe the lessons that present themselves to you, and learn from them as best you can

O notice the emotions that come up as you progress, without letting them interfere with the process

O be aware of how certain possessions make you feel, and, if those feelings aren't positive, allow yourself to discard the items

O forgive yourself if you make mistakes

O be indecisive, as long as you're clear on why

O take as long as you need, knowing that there is no pressure to go any faster

O approach everything with an open mind and an open heart

O let go of any stories you are telling yourself: stories about what your stuff means or how it relates to who you are and where you've been. Our stuff doesn't define us.

Ultimately, we can plan and organise all we like, but nothing will actually change until we dive in and take action. Procrastination is a choice. There will always be unknowns and situations we didn't expect, no matter how prepared we are. That's a good thing! It's all part of the fun, and the learning, and the experience.

Dreams don't work unless you do.

Cut yourself some slack

There's no space for feeling guilty in this journey. Choosing to make changes is the important thing. How we got to the point of needing to make those changes is unimportant. What matters is that we're here now. Put the negativity aside. Know this: it's not our fault that we have too much stuff.

We live in an age when there's more choice and more stuff to buy than ever before. Things are cheaper than they've ever been, we have more disposable income than we've ever had ... and even if we don't actually have the money to buy things, that doesn't stop the banks happily lending it to us anyway. Because of all this choice, we've never had to know our 'enough'. We never stop to ask ourselves if we really need all this stuff, or if it's really worth it, until our homes are full and we realise it is creating clutter, stress, anxiety and even debt. On top of that, clever marketing tells us that the stuff they're selling is the answer to our problems, and if we buy it we will be happier, further fuelling this cycle of anxiety and accumulation.

Now, slowly, we are realising that there has to be another way. We've seen the hardships of not having enough, and we've seen the damage caused by excess. We're only beginning to learn what enough really means, what it looks like, and how it feels.

Remember, deciding to make changes is the most important step of the journey. You're on your way, so cut yourself some slack.

Beginning
Before We Begin

09

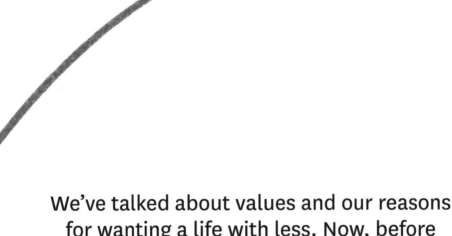

We've talked about values and our reasons for wanting a life with less. Now, before we dive in, let's take some time to connect our hopes and dreams with our reality, and the work we have ahead of us.

Set some time aside to walk through your home, room by room.

○ Notice if the room feels cluttered, or crowded, or open.

○ Look at the stuff you have in each room. Try to remember the last time you noticed or used these items.

○ Ask yourself how you feel as you look around the room. Do you feel stressed or calm, indifferent or pleased?

○ Think about how you'd like the room to be. How would you like it to look, and be used, and how would you like it to feel?

○ Imagine how you'd like it to be when you are finished. Get clear on what you are working towards.

Thinking about how we use our spaces helps us determine what things we need. This sounds obvious, but too often we fill rooms with furniture and 'stuff' just because that's what everybody else does. We don't take the time to think about how *we* use the space, and what is appropriate for us.

The other side to that is whether you are happy with the way the room is used now. Would you prefer it to be used differently? What prevents that from happening? We'll come back to this idea throughout the decluttering process.

During this step, don't make any judgements. Try to remove yourself from the situation. Imagine you are walking through a stranger's home, or that you are a fly on the wall. Be objective. This is not about forming opinions, wishing things were different, or lambasting yourself for things done or choices made in the past. We cannot change the past, and that doesn't matter. We are in control of the present, and that is what determines our future.

Try not to feel overwhelmed. You can do this! There is no rush, and it is not a competition. Remember that you will learn so much through the process and the journey, and the most sustainable outcomes are the ones that take time. Own the situation. Remind yourself why you're doing it. See the opportunity to grow. Embrace the challenge.

If you see items that you already know you do not want, gather them together as you go. There is no need to think this through in detail, or to rummage through your drawers and cupboards searching for things to let go of, as we will go through each room thoroughly later. But if you notice things that you no longer like, have been meaning to get rid of for a while

or didn't even remember you still had,
remove them now. There will be harder
decisions to make later, so clear some
space for these by making the easy ones
now.

Through this process of being aware
of why we are making these changes,
familiarising ourselves with what we need
to do and beginning to find items to let
go, we can start to get a feel for the task
ahead. We can get a feel for the energy
and time that is required. There are no
quick fixes or shortcuts. For almost all
of us, decluttering is a process; the stuff
in our home has accumulated over many
years, often decades, and there may be
several rounds of decluttering before we
find our 'enough'. Our decluttering muscle
gets stronger each time we use it, and our
resolve gets stronger as we begin to see
the results.

Even if your initial walk through your home
identified only a few items to release, or
just a single one, then you are already on
your way. You have begun the journey.
You've taken your first step towards a life
with less. The path to change is through a
series of small steps, one after the other.
Keep going, and you will get there.

Believe it is possible.

Taking Action

10

Getting
Organised

Ready to tackle your stuff? Great ... let's go! As someone who really struggled with decluttering and letting go, believe me, I have tried a lot of methods. I've found there are two schools of thought when it comes to decluttering.

Working on a 'room-by-room' basis can give the instant satisfaction of seeing progress, feeling achievement, and leaving decluttered space in your wake.

When similar items are stored in multiple areas of the house, the 'category-by-category' approach can work better. Grouping items all together can make us aware of how much we own – not so easy when they are spread over several rooms.

While it often creates more mess and chaos before the calm, the category approach leads to more thorough decluttering, in my experience. You don't sort through and make space for things only to later find stuff you'd forgotten about, meaning you need to reorganise; you're far more aware of what you actually own (so you can declutter more effectively); and once a category is done, it's done – you can tick it off!

I find that a combination of category and room-by-room decluttering gives me the best results. If you keep items in multiple places, consider gathering them together and decluttering before you start tackling stuff room by room. The categories will depend on how things are spread out around your home but may include:

○ papers

○ books, newspapers and magazines

○ coats, jackets and outerwear

○ footwear

○ tools and batteries

○ children's toys and games

○ bedding and towels

○ storage containers and servingware.

Ultimately, what works best for you will depend on how much stuff you have, what that stuff is and where you keep it. If you come up with your own ideas as a result of reading this, go ahead and try them. Just because an idea doesn't feature here, it doesn't mean it is not worth giving it a go. There is no one size fits all and there is no single answer.

One thing I will say is, do try everything. Don't just go through the motions – do *all* the work! Keep an open mind and give it your best shot. Rather than thinking, 'This won't work for me', ask yourself if you can make it work for you. Then, once you've tried it, if you still don't like it, or find it unhelpful or stressful, put the idea aside and move on to the next one. Remember, though – you'll never know if it's a good idea until you've actually tried it, and you might be pleasantly surprised.

You can follow the order suggested ahead but might prefer to tackle things in an order that makes more sense for you. You know your home, and the areas needing more work than others. We'll cover how to map out your action plan at the end of this chapter.

Something important to bear in mind: do not start with what you anticipate will be your biggest challenge. There's a good chance you'll feel overwhelmed and defeated before you've even made any real progress. Start with something easy (I always recommend papers).

Setting up a system

Once you make a decision about what should happen to an item, grouping it together with like items reduces double handling, and will make finding new homes for unwanted items a lot more manageable.

You'll need some boxes, at least six. I'm not a fan of plastic sacks. They don't stack, they tear easily and they tend to be used once before heading to landfill (soft black plastic bin liners are unlikely to be recycled, and black plastic is the lowest grade and least valuable of all the colours). Plastic is becoming a huge problem for the environment and these bags represent the convenience-led disposable culture that decluttering and mindful consumption are working to change.

Don't buy new boxes! Repurpose what you have, or head to the supermarket and see if they have any boxes (ask for potato chip or cereal boxes as these are ideal). It's worth using boxes rather than making piles as it's easy to move everything quickly out of your home, and visibility is restricted – making it harder for you to remember what's in there and be tempted to take things back out!

Label the six boxes as follows:

This box is for any item (ideally that is still in good condition and working order) that you will give away – whether to a charity shop, a refuge, a school or someone you know.

Please be respectful! Ensure that anything you donate is clean. If something is faulty, worn and shabby, passing it on to someone else doesn't mean it won't end up in landfill. Charity shops landfill huge amounts of unsellable items every week, and it's an extra cost they don't need to bear.

You may be happy to donate everything you own, but sometimes there is a place for selling. If you're feeling guilty that you spent a lot of money on something you've barely used, selling can be a way to alleviate some of that guilt. If something is rare or valuable, you may prefer to sell it. The same goes for parts and unusual items that probably wouldn't be of use to a charity shop, but will be of use to someone in the world, if you can find them!

This box is for all the items that can be recycled, whether that's in your domestic recycling bin, or at a specialist recycling place for things like electrical waste, batteries, textiles, corks, polystyrene and metals, for example. Lots of things can be recycled; it just requires figuring out where you need to take them or what you need to do. Don't stress about the how – we'll cover this in more detail later. If you think it's recyclable, put it in the box.

This box is for items that need fixing to be usable (and will be worthwhile or simple to fix). That doesn't mean that you have to fix them, just that this is the best option. Consider using this box for items with missing parts, which you want to keep until you've checked the whole house and reunited them with the other part.

Anything not recyclable and beyond repair that no longer appears to have any use to anyone goes here.

You'll note that there is a question mark – don't assume that everything in this box is junk. Before committing the contents to landfill, it is definitely worth checking if any of it is actually recyclable or reusable – we will cover this in the section on taking responsibility for your stuff.

Other

This final box is for anything that you decide to declutter that doesn't fit into the other boxes. It could be items you're undecided on, or still thinking about. It could be items that actually belong to someone else, that you need to return. Or it could be items whose purpose you can't entirely remember, but that you want to put aside in the short term while you try to figure it out.

Six boxes might seem like a lot, but unless you really don't have the space, they will make the decluttering process much more efficient. In fact, you may even find it helpful to add one more box – 'put away', for things you come across that are in the wrong place, or don't have a home. If you have items that shift around from surface to surface because you're not entirely sure where they go, this might be a good opportunity to gather them all together and see if you can find a permanent spot for them. If not, they will need to go into one of the other boxes.

Try to sort your items in batches soon after you do the decluttering work, while you are still in the zone. Once a box is full, or you have a couple of boxes of the same category piling up, act on them. If you deal with items one by one as you find them in your home, the process will take forever. Conversely, if you wait until you have towering stacks of boxes full of stuff to sell or donate, it will feel overwhelming and it's likely you'll put it off. And sorting through boxes again much later means revisiting any emotions you've attached to the items, and increases the chance that you will change your mind. Find your sweet spot.

Mapping out your action plan

A really good way to map out your action plan is to think through all the areas and categories that you need to declutter, and then think about the effort required, and the kind of impact it will have. We'll go through this step by step.

Step one

On the opposite page, you'll find a table. First, in the left column, list all the spaces that need decluttering. Include all the rooms, and don't forget outside spaces too. If you have a lot of stuff and want to divide the rooms into sections to make it more manageable, do it.

In the right column, list all the categories of items (which may be spread over several rooms) that would be good to tackle in one go – rather than having to face them again in every room.

You'll finish with two filled-in columns.

Step two

On page 84, there's a matrix with four boxes. The two boxes on the vertical axis are labelled 'easy' and 'difficult', and the two boxes on the horizontal axis are labelled 'low impact' and 'high impact'. We'll use this grid to help sort your spaces and categories into a plan of action.

Write all the different spaces and categories you listed onto post-it notes (one idea per post-it note) to enable easy sorting. Next, draw the grid out onto a separate piece of paper (butcher's paper or flipchart paper is ideal) or mark out with string on the floor. Then follow step three to fill the matrix.

Spaces	Categories
Home office	*Papers*

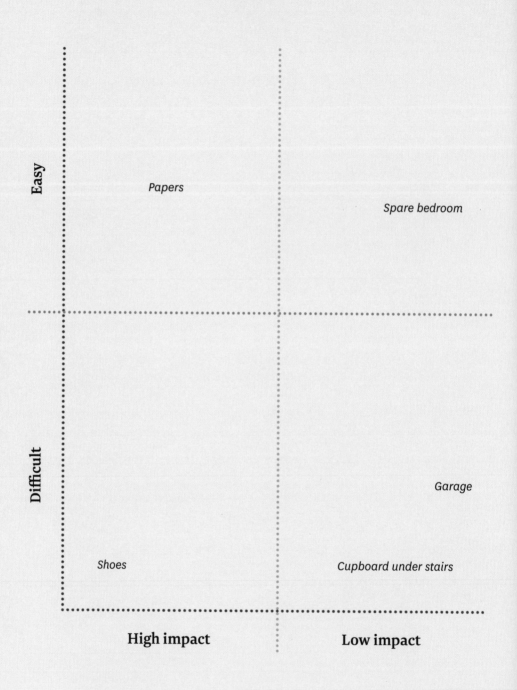

Step three

One by one, go through each post-it note and ask the question: Will I find this space or category hard or easy to declutter? Think about how much attachment you have to the items in this space, how big and full the space is, and how much you think you need to declutter here.

Once you have decided, ask the second question: Will this have a high or low impact? Think about your vision for your home. Is decluttering this space going to have a big impact on that vision, or will it be less noticeable?

Based on your responses, place each space or category somewhere in your grid. Try to avoid placing things on the boundaries! I've got you started with some suggestions on the left, but of course your finished grid will be unique to you. There should be something in each of the four boxes. If everything is in one box, go through everything again and decide which things can be moved across.

Step four

When we make changes, we want to start with what's easiest and we also want to see results quickly, so starting with the things we've classed as easy and high impact makes the most sense. Next, choose the easy things with low impact. This is all practice for the harder stuff! Third, tackle those difficult things with the high impact. Anything that's going to be hard, without much impact, should be left until last. Write down your roadmap in the order you've chosen:

First, I will tackle … (easy, high impact)

....

....

Next, I will move on to … (easy, low impact)

....

....

Third, I'll work on … (difficult, high impact)

....

....

Last, I'll look at … (difficult, low impact)

....

....

Now you have a logical plan of attack.

11

Papers

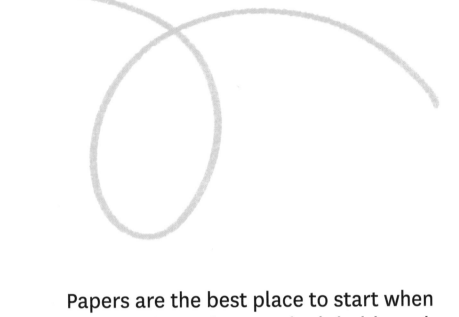

Papers are the best place to start when decluttering. Why? We don't hold much attachment to them (meaning they are easy to get rid of), and you'll notice a difference straightaway. Seeing and feeling success right at the start will give you a big motivation to continue, and you can remind yourself of the feeling when you're dealing with something harder to let go of later on.

Unless filed properly (and seriously, who likes filing?) papers tend to clutter our homes and our surfaces, yet we can never find them when we need them. (Or does that have something to do with the aforementioned lack of filing?) By papers, I'm talking about receipts, bills, invoices, scribbled notes, documents, letters, instruction manuals … Papers are also a great practical introduction to this idea of decluttering by category. They are boring and tedious to sort out, so the idea of having to tackle them again and again in each room is enough to put anyone off decluttering. But getting them out of the way at the start can be a real boost! If this works for you, consider adopting decluttering by category in other areas of the home.

Step one

Gather together all of your papers. ALL of them. Grab any files. Clear your desk and empty any work bags. Remove papers from drawers. Unpin notes from the fridge or pin board. Take any loose papers from surfaces. Check each room and if you see any paper, bring it with you.

Step two

If you have a huge amount of loose papers, you may want to grab a box to keep it all together while you sort. Or you may be happy to spread out. If you find your table too small (and you probably will!) you can either use the floor or work in batches. Choose the method that is best for you. A smartphone or tablet with access to the internet and a pen will also be useful as you work through it all. And get that 'recycle' box ready!

Step three

If you already have files or some kind of filing system, tackle these first to create space. Anything that's no longer useful is going into recycling. If you need to keep documents for tax or other purposes, check how many years you need to keep and discard the old ones; if you don't, choose a timeframe that seems reasonable – possibly the current tax year.

If you know that your bills and documents are available online, maybe you don't need any paper copies at all. If a product is out of warranty, do you still need the receipt? Do you still need the paper instruction manual, or is there a copy available online? (Most electrical-goods manufacturers have downloadable manuals available on their website.) Go through all the papers, one by one, in this way.

Step four

As you go, make piles to file or organise later (keeping it as simple as possible), and try to minimise the paper you hang on to. If you tend to scribble notes on scraps of paper, make one to-do list (ideally an electronic one) and get rid of all the notes. Add events and invites to your calendar. If you're keeping something as a reminder, take a photo.

If you're keeping brochures or magazines for a single article, cut the article out for later. (Warning! Don't try to read it then and there. Tempting as it is, this is procrastination at its finest and it will get in the way of achieving your goals. Save it for later. If you know later is never coming, recycle it now.)

Step five

Once you've gone through everything, don't leave the piles! They will be forgotten and get knocked over and messed up, and you'll have to do the whole thing again. Sort them straightaway, as best you can. If you need to source a couple of extra folders to store it all, make a note (don't rush out to the shops, you've got work to do!) and clip everything together in the meantime.

Step six

Return the newly sorted papers to their homes. If you're not sure where they will be going, place them in the room you think suits, and you can reassess when you come to it later.

Notice the space that you've created. How does it feel? How do *you* feel?

12

Entranceway

This is usually the first space you walk into as you enter the house, and it's the space that others first see when they visit your home. Ask yourself what you use this space for. Is it a transition zone where you prepare for going out into the weather (be it sun, snow or rain)? Is it a place for hanging coats and umbrellas, keeping shoes and reusable shopping bags? Is it a space for storage of other things? Is it an area to drop everything as soon as you enter the front door? How would you like to use this space, and is that different to its current use?

Step one

Start at the top. Remove anything that's hanging: coats, scarves, umbrellas, bags and anything else.

Consider the following questions:

O Which items have been used in the last week/fortnight/month?

O Is there anything here that is broken, or doesn't fit?

O Do you have any similar items that actually serve the same purpose?

O Is there anything that has simply been relegated from the rest of the house – meaning, you actually don't like it much?

If there are things here that you do not use, declutter them. What would be the best outcome for these items – to sell or donate them, or do they need fixing first? Make a choice and place them in the corresponding box, ready to let them go. If there are things you do not use but are reluctant to get rid of, remove them from the entranceway. Place them wherever they belong in the house (so long as this isn't a space that has already been decluttered). Yes, it will mean double handling as you will reassess these items later on, but by the time you revisit them, you may have a different perspective.

Step two

We tend to own multiple pairs of footwear, but we can only wear one pair of shoes at once. Be realistic about which shoes you wear, and which shoes you don't. Unworn shoes deteriorate, so better to pass them on to someone who will wear them now rather than keep them.

Ask the questions:

O How many pairs of shoes have been worn in the last week, and how many have remained unworn for many weeks?

O Do you keep shoes in other places, such as your wardrobe – and are there any shoes sitting here simply waiting to be cleaned and put away?

O Do you have shoes that don't fit, or are uncomfortable, or cause blisters?

O Are there any that need fixing (or are beyond repair), that you don't like, or that don't go with any of your clothes?

If you don't like them, don't wear them or don't have anything to wear them with, let them go. Decide if you'd rather sell or donate them. If they need fixing, put them in the 'repair' box. Set yourself a deadline and if they're not fixed, decide to let them go. That will be the test of whether you really want them.

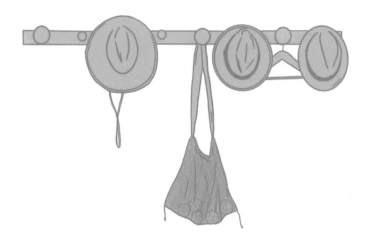

Step three

Pull everything out of any storage and go through item by item. If you don't know what it is or what it's for, don't put it back. Put it in the 'other' box. If you don't remember by the time you're finished, you probably didn't need it in the first place.

Anything that's in the wrong place, put back in the right place (or in the 'put away' box, if you've decided to use one). If you find something you didn't remember you had, or thought you'd got rid of, ask yourself if you really need it.

Step four

Look at your surfaces. Ask whether everything is being used for its intended purpose – for example, chairs are for sitting on, not piling stuff on. If furniture is just gathering clutter, consider removing it or getting rid of it altogether. We often think that more storage will make things tidier, but it just gives us another place to hoard stuff.

Step five

Finally, consider decorative items. If you have plants in your entranceway, check they are alive and pest-free. If you have decorations, are they dust-free? Do you love them, or do you just have them to fill space – or because you didn't know where else to put them? Does cleaning them fill you with joy or with dread? If it's the latter, maybe you should let the item go.

13

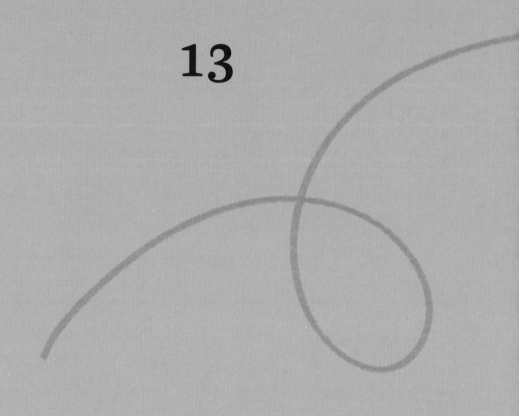

Living Space

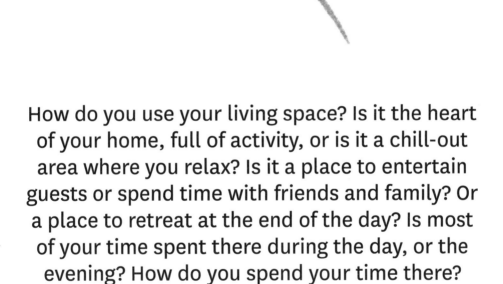

How do you use your living space? Is it the heart of your home, full of activity, or is it a chill-out area where you relax? Is it a place to entertain guests or spend time with friends and family? Or a place to retreat at the end of the day? Is most of your time spent there during the day, or the evening? How do you spend your time there?

Step one

Consider the furniture you own. Do you use it? Do you use it for its intended purpose, and regularly? Is it for special occasions? Is it just another surface to gather unnecessary items? Is it comfortable? Sit on the chairs; open the cupboards and drawers; run your fingers along the shelves.

Removing excess seating is the best way to free up space in your living area. Removing surfaces is the best way to get rid of clutter, and the easiest way to reduce how much time you spend dusting and tidying. Flag items to sell or donate (they'll be too big to put in a box, but make a choice and pop a note in the corresponding box instead).

Step two

Look at your bookshelves. Take each book in turn, and ask yourself: Do I love this book? Do I refer to it regularly? Only keep books that you love and know you will read over and over again. If you own books that you haven't read, but can't bear to part with, put them aside and set a deadline. Tell yourself that they are leaving your home once the deadline is reached, whether you've read them or not. In the future, there might be far better books on the same topic – why hold on to the ones you have now? If you still want to read a book down the line, you can always borrow it from the library when you're ready. Remember, being well read has absolutely nothing to do with how many books you own.

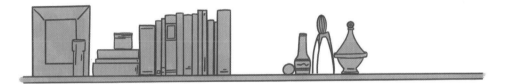

Step three

Look at the stacks of CDs or records that you have. How many have remained unplayed in years? Only keep music that you play constantly. Consider uploading music to your computer or exploring a digital music subscription service and selling, donating or recycling the CDs.

Step four

Do you have a DVD tower full of DVDs you've only watched once? Take each disc and ask yourself: When was the last time I watched this? Can you imagine yourself watching it again? Is it available at the library, or via file-lending services? Only keep DVDs that you watch regularly; commit to selling, donating or recycling the rest.

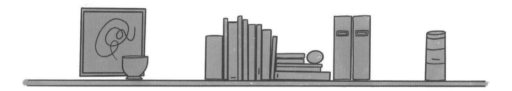

Step five

Do you have unread magazines building up in the corner? Do you have past issues that you know you'll never refer back to? Only keep magazine subscriptions if you can't wait to read the latest edition and always read it cover to cover. With the copies that you have, remove articles you want to keep and donate or recycle the rest. Even better, take photos of the bits you want to keep, and then donate the (still-intact) magazines. You can also check the internet to see if there's an online version of the article you like and bookmark it.

Step six

What about the ornaments that line your shelves and cabinets, and any artwork that hangs on your walls? How do you feel when you see it? How do you feel when you hold it? Do you keep these pieces because you love them, or because they fill the space, or because you somehow acquired them?

If you don't love them, they only serve to collect dust and create more work for you. Decide how you will let them go.

Step seven

Open up any cabinets and cupboards, and pull out the contents. All of it. Touch everything. If you don't know what something is, or didn't remember you had it, decide how you want to get rid of it. Don't give yourself time to reattach to things you'd already forgotten about.

Anything you can't remember using recently, consider letting go. Anything quirky but impractical, any novelty items that remain unused – don't allow them to take up space. Someone else might really want those items! Remove any duplicates. If you're storing items in dark cupboards where they can't be seen or remembered, the chances are you don't need or want them.

14

Dining Area

Do you use this area every day, or is there a separate place where you tend to eat most of your meals, meaning the designated dining area is left for 'special occasions'? If so, how regular are these occasions? Regular enough to justify owning a whole separate set of furniture?

Step one

How many chairs do you own, and do you use all of them for seating, or are some used for storage and collecting 'stuff' instead? How many chairs do you own that live elsewhere in your home – could these be used for those events where you need extra seating, rather than the ones that stay in your dining area? Sit on the chairs – are they comfortable? Choose to let go of any chairs you don't use.

How do you *feel* when you sit at the table? Is your furniture too big for what you need or too small to be useful? If it's not serving the purpose for which it is meant, consider removing it from your home altogether. Decide whether you'd prefer to sell or donate it, and pop a note in the corresponding box.

Step two

Take everything out of your drawers and cupboards. If you keep cutlery, crockery and glassware here as well as the kitchen, you may find it useful to combine it all to see how much you truly own. (Whether you do this now or wait until you tackle the kitchen is your choice – it is your home, and you know it best.)

If you have multiple place settings, ask yourself which one is used most often. Why is that? What are the other sets for, and how often do you use them? Keeping sets for 'best' is a waste of resources. Keeping many sets when you have a small household and rarely entertain large numbers of guests is unnecessary.

Count how many forks, knives and spoons you own. Count how many plates and bowls. Count all the different glasses. Do you use all the types of glasses, or do you stick to a certain style? What about serving platters, bowls and condiment dishes? Remember, all of that has to be washed up, perhaps dried and even polished, and put away. How many do you use regularly? How many do you use when you have guests? What is the maximum you'd ever need? What could you get by without? Look for items that can have multiple uses, and consider letting go of those items with just a single specific purpose.

Step three

Do you have table linen and placemats?
Go through each item. Are any damaged,
stained or soiled to the point where you
tend not to use them? Do you keep table
linen that is too small or large for your
table? Do you have anything you are
reluctant to use because it is difficult
to clean? What about novelty items that
are only used once a year? Do you really
need different linen or place settings for
a single day? Consider anything you have
multiples of and ask yourself if they are
really necessary. Can you make do with
a single set, or two at most?

15

Kitchen

Kitchens are a mass of cupboards and shelves with storage galore. If the thought of tackling the whole kitchen at once is overwhelming, split it up into categories: bakeware, crockery, gadgets, or whatever works for you. And we'll get to food in the next chapter. Be mindful of your fantasy self in the kitchen – is it actual you who loves baking, can't wait to knock up a freshly squeezed juice and adores throwing dinner parties, or is it fantasy you?

Step one

Before tackling the cupboards and shelves, start with everything already out in the open. Begin at the top, and work down. Consider any hanging utensils or cookware. Remove anything and everything that is hanging up, and go through each item one by one. Why is it here? Is it useful? Do you love it? Do you use it? Or is it clutter that has somehow accumulated here?

Fridge magnets are clutter that enable us to pin more clutter to the fridge. Unless you truly love them, let them go. If your pin board is cluttered, remove some of the pins – that way you will be more ruthless with what you pin there.

How many tea towels hanging on your hooks are dirty? We can only use one tea towel at once, so having several on display creates clutter – and it's hard to tell which is new (and which is dirty) when there are several. Do you even need to own so many? Ask the same questions about aprons. Textiles can be donated if in good condition, or otherwise recycled.

Are your artworks tired and greasy, or do you love them and clean them? Do you use your wall calendar, or is it two months behind? If you don't use it, recycle it.

Step two

What's on your windowsill or countertops? If you have plants, are they healthy, or breeding aphids and vinegar flies? Do you have random bits of junk that you don't know what to do with? If it's broken, put it in the 'repair' box, make a note to find out how to fix it, and remove from the counter. If it belongs somewhere else, move it there (or place in the 'put away' box).

Step three

Do you keep anything on the floor, besides your bin? Recycling bottles, dustpan and brush, shoes … Gather everything and either put it away or ask yourself if there's a better place it can go. If there's no room in your cupboards (yet), put it in the 'other' box until you find space.

Step four

Empty all your drawers and cupboards. If you've already gone through your tableware and servingware, you can leave these, but another round doesn't hurt – and if not, include them now, along with all your cooking utensils, cookware, saucepans and bakeware.

Don't forget about hanging utensils or cookware that you considered in step one – duplicates may be hidden in cupboards. Organise everything by category if this helps you break it down, then go through each group item by item.

With each group, pick out your favourites – the things you use every day, that are the perfect size or the perfect fit for your needs. Then consider everything else. Anything that you dislike or never use, or cannot remember the last time that you used, remove immediately. Will you sell, donate or recycle them?

Look at what's left. How many duplicates do you have? How many less-than-ideals? What do you have that you know you could do without? Are there any tools that can take the place of other tools, or any dishes that can do the work of other dishes? Is there anywhere else you can simplify?

Ask yourself how many of each item is practical for you. If you only have a four-ring cooktop, owning more than four saucepans probably makes little sense. If you rarely bake, owning all the baking tin shapes is unlikely to be necessary. If you have an electric whisk and a fork, do you need the hand whisk too?

Step five

Finally, pull everything out from the cupboard under the sink. It's the same drill. If it's useful, keep it. (If it's beautiful, keep it too, but question why you're keeping it under the sink if it's truly beautiful!) If it's broken, old, unnecessary, unwanted, hazardous to your health … decide on the best way to let it go.

16

Pantry and Fridge

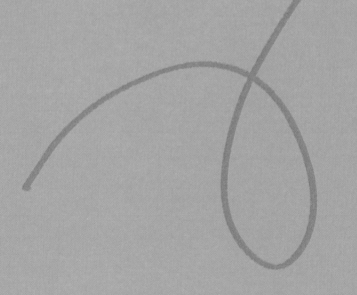

Pantries and fridges benefit from a declutter as much as cupboards and drawers. Unidentified packets at the back of the shelf, or jars that we're afraid to open for fear of what's inside, have no place in our homes. Now is the time to take stock, remove the long-expired items and make plans to use up what's been sitting around a little too long.

Step one

Remove all the food items from your pantry. Every single jar, packet and tin, no matter how small. If you have food in any other cupboards or on the counter, add it to the stockpile.

Step two

Now, one by one, go through and check for signs of spoilage and the use-by and best-before dates. A use-by date indicates the expiration date of a product, and tells us the last day this product is safe to consume. On the other hand, a best-before date tells us the last day that the food is considered to be perfect; after this date it may just lose its freshness, taste, aroma or nutrients, but it is still safe to eat.

Anything that has exceeded its use-by date should be discarded. Anything that has exceeded its best-before date can be kept if it seems to be in good condition, if you know you will use it.

Step three

Make a note of any products that are close to their use-by date, or past or close to their best-before date; later, you can search for recipes to help you use them up. Put a reminder in your calendar so you can meet the deadline.

Make a note too of anything you have lots of so you can plan ahead to begin using it up. If you have an obscure ingredient that you know you won't use in time, consider if anyone you know might want to use it.

Step four

Once you've sorted through everything, decant any open packets of food into glass jars or see-through containers, if you have them. Food items will keep better in sealed containers than open packets; they will also stack better and it is far easier to see what you have. If you don't have enough containers, prioritise the things that are more likely to go stale. Cut off the label with the name and expiry and pop into the jar so you know what it is, and place the packaging aside for recycling. If you find multiples of the same thing, consider combining them.

Step five

Now pull everything (yes, everything) out of the refrigerator and freezer. Give the empty fridge a good clean (or at least a wipe). Check best-before and use-by dates and for signs of spoilage as you put things back in. If a product is in a glass jar or container, open it up to check it's still okay. Discard anything old, unidentifiable or bad. Again, make a note in your calendar to use up anything close to expiry.

When it comes to discarding spoiled food, you might want to look into backyard compost or community compost options – composting food waste is one of the best ways to reduce what you send to landfill.

17

Laundry and Linen Cupboard

If you have a separate laundry room,
you'll probably find that this is where stuff you
don't actually need or use seems to accumulate.
If you don't have a separate laundry room,
you'll have a head start!

The laundry is where we clean our clothes, yet we often combine this with some of the dirtiest things in the house: muddy boots, outdoors equipment and pet food. Sometimes this is intentional – but not always. Think about how you'd like this room to be used. Are you happy combining the clean and dirty? Would you rather separate the two? What would your ideal space look like and how would it work for you? What changes can you implement to make that a reality?

Step one

If there are any clothes in the laundry, they need to be sorted before you begin. If you have any dirty laundry, do what you need to do – put them in the washing machine, or handwash them if you need to. If you have clothes that are really difficult to wash and tend to languish in your washing basket, perhaps you should let them go.

Anything clean, put away (or place in the 'put away' box for later). For anything awaiting mending, ask yourself how long it has been there. Will you actually mend it yourself, or are you willing to take it somewhere to be mended? Make a decision now – to repair, repurpose or donate it. If you decide to mend it, set yourself a deadline and stick to it.

Do the same for anything that needs ironing – consider how long it's been waiting. If you really dislike ironing, maybe you should declutter any items that need to be ironed. Anything that is in the 'too hard' basket needs to go in the 'donate' box.

Step two

Once clothes are sorted, start from the top and work down. Remove anything hanging from the walls or hooks. Is it clean, is it useful and is it used? Do you love it? Do you need it? Could you do without it? Choose now: sell, donate or recycle.

Step three

Gather everything on the counters or other surfaces. If there's anything that should be in the cupboards, put it away. Look at what's left. Are there duplicates or things you never use? Do you have multiples of anything that you could do without?

Step four

Open up the cupboards and drawers and pull everything out. Any bottles or jars, packets, lotions or potions: consider them one by one. Remove anything expired or that you doubt you'll need again any time soon. If you're not sure, take that as a yes

and remove it. (Important – don't pour anything down the sink! Put the containers in the 'other' box to take to a hazardous chemicals collection point later.) If there's anything useful and in good condition that you won't use, consider donating it.

Open the lids to check for spoilage, and to make sure that none of the containers are empty or practically empty. Combine any duplicates, and if there's anything that's really really old – or unidentifiable – then get rid of it.

Step five

Tackle the linen cupboard – the place where you store towels and bedding. Pull everything out, and open all your bedsheets and towels. Run your fingers over the fabric. Put them close to your nose and smell them. Do they seem fresh and new, or are they tatty, stained or worn? Do they have holes? When was the last time you used them?

How many sets do you own, and how many do you use? Accounting for visitors, what is the maximum you'd need? Can you get by with less? Are there any that you dislike, or that are uncomfortable, hard to clean or an impractical size? If things need washing to refresh them, add them to the laundry basket. For items you no longer want, separate into 'repair', 'donate' and 'recycle'.

Step six

Last, check the floor. Are you storing things on the floor? Had you even noticed that they were there? Can they fit somewhere else, or do you need them at all?

Bathroom and Toilet

18

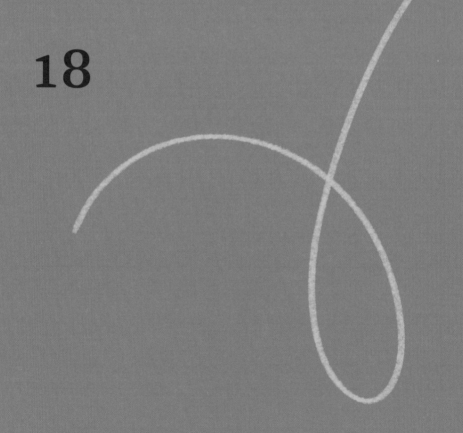

It is surprising how much clutter accumulates in bathrooms, most of it disguised as 'useful' stuff … that we don't actually use. As in the kitchen, this is one area where it pays to gather things of the same category together so you can see just what you've been stockpiling, starting with what's out in the open.

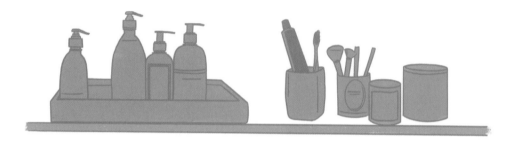

Step one

First, inspect any decorations you have in the bathroom. What is their purpose, and do they serve this purpose well? Are the pictures beautiful, and the plants healthy? Do you enjoy looking at them, or do you feel indifferent? Are they here simply because you felt the need to put them somewhere, and so they ended up in the bathroom? Are any ornaments or trinkets clean, or are they dusty? How do you feel about having to dust them? Which things do you love, and which ones are not important to you? Use these questions to decide if they stay or go.

Step two

What about towels, washcloths and bath mats? Are there more than you need? Old textiles can be donated or recycled.

Step three

Gather all your electronic gadgets: foot spas, shavers, epilators, electric toothbrushes, hairdryers, hair straighteners, hair curlers, fragrance burners – anything with a plug. Which of these things do you use, and which of these things sit around collecting dust? When was the last time you used them? Do you really need them, or are they just clutter? Sell, donate or recycle.

Step four

What about non-consumables – scissors, tweezers, nail files, soap dishes or dispensers, mirrors, combs, hairbrushes, exfoliating brushes, sponges?

Remove every single one of these items from bathroom surfaces and go through them one by one. Is there anything here that you don't even use? Are there any duplicates – and do you need them? Could one thing serve the purpose of several? Is anything too tatty, or broken? Put anything that can be decluttered into the appropriate box.

Step five

Consumables are things like shampoo, conditioner, soap, shower gel, lotions and creams, make-up, perfume and toothpaste that we use up over time. Remove them all from the shower, the bath and the basin and put them together. Which things do you use regularly, and which things do you not use at all? Are any of the bottles empty? Anything you do not like or do not use, remove now. Unopened and barely used products can be donated; most packaging can be recycled.

Step six

There should be nothing left on your counters or surfaces. If there's anything remaining, remove these things too, and ask yourself if you need them.

Step seven

Now, open your cupboards and drawers and pull everything out. Are there any duplicates of the things you've already been through? If you're keeping any replacement items, can you see yourself needing them in the next six months? If not, they are 'just in case' items and it might be better to let them go.

With the items you don't use, what are you saving them for? Do you know how long you've had them? Can you imagine yourself using them? Do they have expiry dates, and have they expired? With spares and refills, how long do you expect them to last? Could you donate any and free up some space?

Take stock of everything you're storing and make a note not to succumb to any more supermarket specials or pharmacy '3 for 2' offers until these are used up!

Look at the medicines. Have any expired? Have any outlived their purpose? Are any unlabelled? Remove anything that you don't need now and don't consider to be an essential. If you have a first aid kit, look

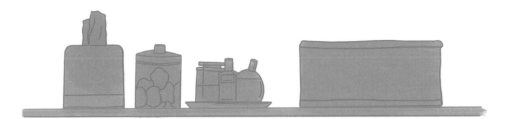

in there too. Is anything damaged, worn, broken or expired?

With make-up, perfume and toiletries, ask yourself how old they are and when you last used them. Open them up: Are they still in good condition? Can you think of an occasion coming up where you'll use them? Look at the ingredients: Are they the kinds of ingredients you want to be putting onto your skin, and breathing in? How do you feel when you use them?

Anything old, that you don't wear, don't like or (admit it) doesn't actually suit you, let it go. If you don't feel comfortable using it, let it go. The packaging is probably recyclable, even if the contents aren't. Do you feel the pull to try to use something up rather than let it go? Ask yourself why you haven't used it up before. (Maybe it has been lurking at the back of a drawer, forgotten until now. Maybe it just isn't something you actually want to use.)

Step eight

Now begin putting things back, starting with the things you use all the time, and the things you use often. Put back a single spare of anything you use regularly. Rehang the towels. Look at what's left. Give yourself another chance to let go of anything you know is not truly useful before you put the rest of the things back in their place.

Bedroom

19

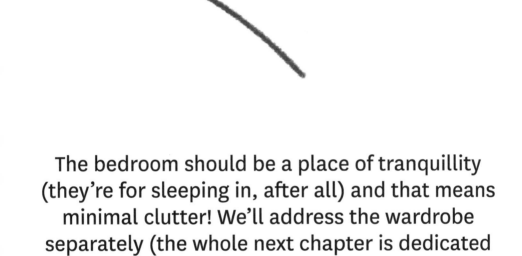

The bedroom should be a place of tranquillity (they're for sleeping in, after all) and that means minimal clutter! We'll address the wardrobe separately (the whole next chapter is dedicated to it). First we will focus on the rest of the clutter that gathers in our bedroom.

Ask yourself how the bedroom currently makes you feel, and how you'd like it to make you feel. How you want to feel when you wake up in the morning or when you go to bed at night? How do your possessions stop you feeling that way? Can you store any (useful) items elsewhere? As you remove items from the bedroom, notice how your feelings change. Notice how your perceptions of the room and the energy in it change. Do you notice that as you remove the clutter the room feels calmer? Can you feel the space that you're creating?

Step one

Start by picking all your clothes up off the floor, the bed, the back of the chair and anywhere else they might be, and either put them away (ready for the wardrobe declutter) or put them in the laundry. Next, make the bed.

Apologies if you're someone who never leaves their clothes on the floor and always makes the bed – at least you have a head start. Creating order and calm is the first step in visualising what an uncluttered bedroom looks like – and what it feels like.

Step two

If you have under-bed storage (that isn't used to store clothing) pull it out. It's a good opportunity to give under the bed a quick vacuum and dust off all the boxes. Before you open them, ask yourself if can you even remember what you stored here. If you don't know and don't want to know, remove them from the bedroom immediately. If you can't take such drastic action (I couldn't!), one by one, open them. Take everything out and hold it in your hands. What items are you storing? When you see them, how do you feel? Are you pleased or do you feel an extra weight on your shoulders? If you didn't remember owning it, it isn't useful and it doesn't fill you with joy, choose a box and let it go.

Step three

Work your way through all the non-clothing storage in your bedroom. Clear all the surfaces and empty all the drawers, and look at each item individually. Anything that you use regularly, and anything that you absolutely love, put back. Consider what's left. If you keep a lot of make-up or toiletries in your bedroom, you may want to consider collecting what you have in the bathroom and sorting it by category.

Step four

Look at the decorations in the room. Do they make you smile, or are you fed up with them? Do you notice them, or had you forgotten that they were there? How do they make you feel? If they are tired, dusty or you no longer notice them, maybe their useful life in your home has ended.

20

Wardrobe

Wardrobes ideally only contain clothes that actually fit, that we actually like and wear. Sometimes, there is a whole heap of extra baggage (in the form of guilt and wistfulness) hanging in our closets. If you have anything in your wardrobe that you're hoping to slim back into, or hoping to someday have another occasion to wear it to, this might apply to you. From a recovering wardrobe hoarder, know this: you need to make peace with the way you are now, and remove these things from your life.

Deciding what we like is the first step to decluttering our wardrobe, but having an effective wardrobe isn't just about what we like. It's as much about what we actually wear. These might seem like the same thing, but they are not. Clothing, jewellery and other accessories are meant to be worn. We can appreciate the design, the material, the colour and the style, but if we're not wearing it, do we really love it? Or do we just love the idea of it?

I know it's not technically a room (for most people), but the wardrobe can be a very difficult job in the decluttering journey. Because of that, I recommend a more comprehensive two-step process. First we need to remove the things we know we don't wear or don't like. Next we can test whether we wear the things that remain, and explore what our ideal wardrobe really looks like. It is likely that you won't achieve wardrobe perfection (if perfection is even a thing) at your first attempt. In reality, it might take several rounds to get closer to your ideal, so don't panic. And a note: you're going to need an extra box for this process.

Step one

Remove *every single item of clothing you own* from your wardrobe and shelves, as well as those items hanging behind the door, languishing in the laundry basket and generally distributed about your home. You can keep them on the hangers if it's simpler.

Move your clothing into another room: it will help you think more objectively. You might think it would be easier to just look at everything hanging on a rail and make choices from there. Easier maybe, but physically moving your things is so much more effective. After all, you open your wardrobe seven days a week and gaze inside to find something to wear. This needs to feel different if you want to take action.

In a separate space, you can be really clear about *exactly* what you own. Nothing is hidden behind anything else, and it's harder to ignore something when it is in your hands – you can't miss it, or skim over it. You can also group things together so you can see exactly *how many* of every different type of item you own. Plus, physically moving everything makes you realise how much you have. Clothing is surprisingly heavy – actually lifting and feeling them is much more powerful than glancing at a rail of hanging items.

Choose a room with enough space to spread everything out. Laying a sheet out on the floor in the living room creates a space to work from; alternatively, if you have a spare bedroom with a bed, this might be easier. If you only have a small space, you can pile everything onto your bed and carry items to the other room category by category.

Divide your clothing into categories. You may not need all of the ones suggested below, or you may find it helpful to combine some of them. On the other hand, you may need to sub-divide some further to make them more manageable. Do what works best for you.

○ underwear (including undergarments, tights, swimwear and nightwear)

○ casual tops (T-shirts and vest tops)

○ smart tops (shirts and blouses)

○ jumpers and cardigans

○ shorts and cropped trousers

○ exercise and loungewear

○ skirts

○ dresses

○ trousers and jeans

○ work attire (anything that you wear solely for work, including suits)

○ outerwear (jackets, coats, hats, gloves)

○ shoes

○ accessories (bags, belts and jewellery)

○ other.

Working through each category one at a time, lay everything out. Notice the weight of your clothing as you carry it. Look at the items in front of you. Do you notice a type of item that you have a lot of – and more than you need? Are there two or more items that are remarkably similar and do you need both? You may not have realised that you own thirty-five pairs of socks, or that you have four grey jumpers that are surprisingly alike. When things are hanging or folded in the closet, it's hard for us to truly visualise what we own.

One by one, consider each item, and ask yourself: Do I love it? Does it fit? When was the last time I wore it? Can I think of a time in the near future when I'll wear it again? What are the reasons I don't wear it? Does it need repairing, or do I have nothing that matches? Is it inappropriate for the weather? Is it too dressy or too casual to be of real use?

Finally, ask whether it deserves a place in your closet.

There are three possible answers:

○ If it's a 'no', place in the decluttering pile, for donating, selling, repairing or recycling.

○ If it's a firm 'yes', place in a pile to go back in the wardrobe.

○ If it's a less firm yes, or a 'maybe', put it to one side.

Once you've sorted through all your categories, come back to your 'maybe' pile and dig a little deeper with those questions. If you don't love it, it doesn't fit and you don't wear it all the time, think hard about *why* you want to keep it. What are you holding on to it for? Are you projecting thoughts of how you'd like yourself or your life to be (your fantasy self) onto your clothing? Are you hoping for a time when you lose weight, or restart an exercise regime, or get invited to more weddings, or get that promotion at work? Remember, guilt is not a reason to keep stuff you don't need and don't wear.

If you genuinely believe that you will lose weight, get a promotion or be partying every weekend, then put those items aside in an extra box – this will be your 'wait-and-see' box. Keep sorting through your 'maybe' pile until you decide 'yes', 'no' or 'wait-and-see'.

You should be left with two piles of clothes and a box.

The 'no' pile is the stuff that you'll be letting go of. Remove these items from the bedroom and split them between the relevant boxes: 'donate', 'sell', 'repair' or 'recycle'.

The 'yes' pile contains the items that you want to keep, that you feel you wear often and like. Place these back in the wardrobe.

The 'wait-and-see' box should be sealed, labelled with the date and put aside to store. Whatever you do, don't put these items back in the wardrobe. Give yourself a timeframe: three months, or six months, or whatever works for you. If you really mean to change, you've set yourself a realistic goal. When the time comes, it will already be decided if these things are necessary or not.

Step two

Now you've gone through a round of decluttering and everything you want to keep is back in the wardrobe, tie a scarf to one end of your wardrobe rail. It doesn't matter if it is left or right, but for the purposes of explaining, let's choose the left side. Over the next three to six months you will monitor what you actually wear. Set a timeframe that you think is reasonable and practical – I would recommend the same one you've chosen for your wait-and-see box. Whatever timeframe you choose, it helps to think seasonally as weather affects what we wear. Pop the date in your calendar so you don't forget.

At the beginning, all of your clothes will be hanging in the wardrobe to the right of the scarf. As you wear things, return them to the wardrobe but hang them on the other (left) side of the scarf. Wear things as you normally would. It is fine to take things from the left and wear them again; just continue to place them back on the left. However, things *can only cross from the right-hand side to the left-hand side once they have been worn.*

At the end of your chosen timeframe, everything that you have worn will be on one side of the wardrobe rail, to the left of the scarf, and everything you haven't worn will be on the other side of the rail, to the right of the scarf. If every single item has been worn, the scarf will now be at the far right of the rail. More likely, it will be sitting somewhere in the middle.

What is hanging to the left of your scarf, and what is hanging on the right? Count how many items you actually wore. The number you wore will give you an idea of how many items you truly need in your closet. We often think that more clothes equals more choice, and yet we tend to wear the same few outfits over and over. We don't need nearly as much choice as we think we do, and visualising it is the best way to realise that.

The items you've worn and the items you haven't worn will tell you a lot about yourself: the styles and the colours that you prefer, the things in your wardrobe that are more versatile and which are the least, the items you truly love and keep going back to and the things that you actually never quite get around to putting on.

Ask yourself truthfully why you didn't wear an item. Just because you haven't worn something, it doesn't mean you don't need it. You might have jumpers unworn because it has been a hot summer, or exercise gear that you didn't wear because you've been recovering from an injury. But if it's because it doesn't fit or isn't comfortable, let it go.

Now go back to your 'wait-and-see' box. Ask yourself – did your plans eventuate? If not, you can let it go. You don't need it.

Once you've finished, if you still feel like there's work to do, remove all of your clothes from the rail, and begin the process again.

This method doesn't need to be limited to your hanging space. You could use a similar system with other clothing storage – say, moving things from one drawer, shelf or jewellery holder to another as you wear them.

If this two-step approach works well for you and you are struggling to declutter another area of your house – say kitchen appliances, or make-up – you may even want to try and replicate the process with that area. Move your kitchen appliances from one side of the cupboard to another, place a marker on your bookshelf, or move make-up into a new drawer.

It surprised me that each time I decluttered my wardrobe, the number of things I let go of increased, even though the overall number of items I owned decreased. I expected it to be harder, but it got easier. That is because I was finally learning what things I liked and wore, and were useful, and which things were not. Embracing a second round of wardrobe decluttering is a great chance to really test your 'enough' … and end up with a smaller wardrobe full of items that you love to wear. No more stress in the morning as you struggle to pull an outfit together. Less really is more!

Wardrobe stumbling blocks

If you're struggling to declutter your wardrobe and you're not quite sure why, maybe you can relate to these excuses.

I'll slim back into clothes that used to fit.

Of course this could be true. But I'd been telling myself that I was going to slim into my clothes for three years. I'd set myself a three-month deadline, fail to meet it, and extend it by another three months. The truth is, I wasn't increasing my exercise or giving up chocolate, and, when it came down to it, I didn't really want to put in the work. My weight was unlikely to change. If it did, would I even want to wear those clothes that had been languishing in my wardrobe for years? Why allow myself to be reminded of what I hadn't achieved every single time I opened my wardrobe doors?

It might come in handy one day.

The real question is: Why don't I wear it now? I found that my reasons included owning something similar that I preferred, lack of comfort, inappropriateness for the weather, or impracticality. In the past I've been guilty of keeping items of clothing for the time when other preferred garments wear out, and I've learned that well-made clothes take a surprisingly long time to wear out. Would

I even want to wear that garment that had sat untouched and unloved? Uncomfortable clothes rarely (or ever) become comfortable. The weather is unlikely to change much (if there are no plans to relocate), and the clothes I own need to be practical for where I live and what I do now.

I'll never get back what I paid for it, so getting rid of it would be a waste of money.

I have purchased items that I then haven't worn, or have only worn a handful of times. Some of these items were expensive to buy, and others had taken a while to track down, so I didn't want to feel that I'd wasted my time or money, and I kept them. The truth is, I *had* wasted my time and money. I wasted it the moment I made the purchase. Whether the item sat in my wardrobe or was given away didn't change the fact that I'd made a poor choice – it happens, and we've all done it! But rather than forgiving myself for making a poor choice, I'd keep the item hanging there, unworn. It didn't persuade me to wear it. It simply reminded me every time I opened my wardrobe that I'd wasted my money, and left me feeling guilty.

If I could find the right shoes/haircut/ accessories, it would suit me.

I kept items that didn't really suit me because I loved the look of them. I loved the fabric, or the design, or the colour – but sadly it didn't love me back. I was holding on to this idea of the me who looked good in these clothes – my fantasy self. However, the reality was, while they looked great on the model in the catalogue, or in the shop, they weren't flattering and didn't suit my skin tone, body shape or age. Loving the style (or the design, or the brand) doesn't always translate into wearability.

I hate waste, and getting rid of stuff is a waste.

This was the excuse I struggled with most. I'd justify keeping things that I didn't wear because I 'didn't want them to go to waste'. But the idea that by sitting in my home unused they were not going to waste was crazy! If I could donate or sell them, that was a far better use of resources. As for the really tatty stuff: well, at some stage clothes do wear out. Personally, I'm happy to darn holes and wear old clothes, but there comes a point when I start to feel miserable and frumpy. For me, that's when they have to go. I have to let them go. Keeping them and hating them is not healthy, nor is it helpful (and they don't get worn). It's fine to have a set of old ugly clothes for the garden (if you actually garden) but there's no need to have a wardrobe full of them. That still doesn't mean they need to be binned: they can be cut up into rags for cleaning, composted or recycled.

Home Office

21

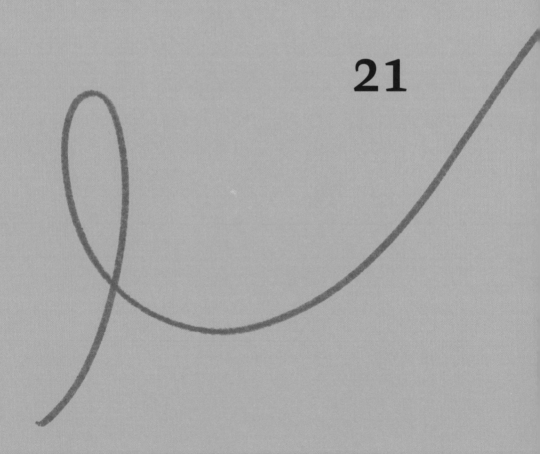

What role does your office space play in your life? How often do you use the space, and at what time of day? Do you work from home and use it for business purposes? Do you use it for household or general admin, for research or for unwinding? Is it a place to study or to do homework? Is it a place to play computer games or to browse the internet? Do you use a desktop computer or a laptop? Or do you use both – and if so, which do you prefer? Do you prefer to sit here to use a screen, or would you rather take your laptop to a different room?

Offices are usually places where we go because we need to 'get stuff done'. Is this true for you? If so, you can increase your productivity by keeping distractions to a minimum. Clutter is a distraction. The less clutter, the calmer the space and the more conducive it is to working effectively.

Step one

Thinking about how you spend your time in this space, consider all the 'equipment' you keep here. How much of it is really useful, and how much is here collecting dust just because it's something that 'all home offices should have'? Do you really need a printer, a scanner, a set of speakers, a video cam, or any of the gadgets you have sitting on your desk or shelves? How often do you use each item? Are you confident that it actually works? Can you make use of the local library instead, or do you have access at work to some of these tools? Do you have neighbours or friends you could ask in an emergency (if there even is such a thing as a 'printing' or 'scanning' emergency)? Anything you can do without, commit to the 'sell', 'donate' or 'recycle' boxes.

Step two

Clear everything from your desk, open all the drawers and remove the contents. Look at each item and ask: Do I need it? If these things are cluttering your workspace, they aren't making you more organised – they are making you less organised.

○ If there are any loose cables and you have no idea what they are for, put them in the 'other' box. Once you've worked through the whole house, if you still cannot identify them, they can be recycled.

○ If you have filled-in notebooks, ask yourself honestly if you'll ever refer to them, and consider recycling them.

○ Any stationery that you no longer use, remove and place in the 'donate' box. Any multiples, remove. If you don't need them, donate them.

○ Any consumables (staples, pens, envelopes, sticky tape, notebooks) that you know you won't use within six months, remove (if six months isn't an appropriate timeframe for you, choose what works better). Even seemingly insignificant things like bulldog clips and elastic bands: if you don't use them, donate them.

○ Any novelty items that are a distraction (and which the novelty has worn off), remove and place in the appropriate box.

Put back only what you need and use regularly.

Step three

Go through the rest of your storage. If you have blank CDs or DVDs, or USB drives, check the contents. Do you need them? Can you save the files to a single hard drive and donate or recycle the storage devices?

Step four

What about shelves and filing cabinets? Do you have any files filled with documents you no longer use (and that you didn't clear back in the 'papers' step)? If you know you're unlikely to look at them again, let them go. If you no longer remember what they are, let them go. If you're in any doubt at all, let them go! The paper can be recycled and storage folders donated.

22

Shed and Garage

The shed and the garage are designed to store bicycles, cars and other machinery, outside equipment, tools, and the accessories that relate to these. This might include sports equipment, gardening tools or camping gear. They are not really intended to be overspill storage for stuff we'd like to keep in the house but no longer fits. If we don't like a possession, don't treasure it and/or don't value it enough to keep it in the house (if that's where it should be), then we probably shouldn't own it at all.

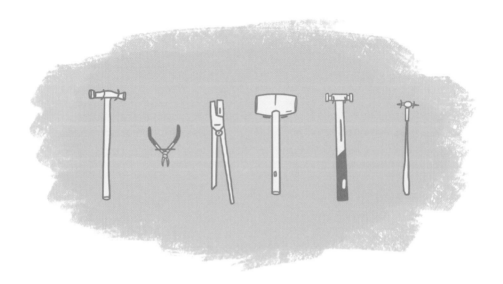

Step one

Work through these spaces item by item, asking yourself: Is this something that truly belongs here? If you cannot answer 'yes', assign it to the 'other' box while you deal with the stuff that does belong here.

If you come across boxes still sealed from the last time you moved house (and that was more than three months ago) consider assigning them to the 'donate' box without opening them at all.

Step two

For those things that you consider do belong in the shed or garage, ask yourself when was the last time that you used them. Garages and sheds might be a great place to store hobby stuff, but the real question is whether all of it is actually used. We sometimes mistake our desire to be good at something or to have a skill as the desire to learn it – and they are not the same thing at all. Wanting something is not the same as actually doing something about it.

If you come across anything that you plan to use in the future, can you schedule a time in your calendar to actually begin to use it? Or is it too far into the future? In that case, you're better off letting it go. When the distant future arrives, you'll be able to get replacement equipment. Equipment stored in sheds and garages rarely improves with age.

Just because you use something occasionally, that doesn't mean that you should keep it. Why do you use it only occasionally? To keep someone else happy? Because you'd like to enjoy it, but when you use it you realise it's not as much fun as you thought? If you have several hobbies, you might find that choosing to let some go means you free up more time, space and energy for the ones you really love.

Step three

As you progress, check things work, have all their parts and, if they contain batteries, check that the batteries are not leaking.

Step four

If you have any vehicles in your garage, declutter the insides of these too. Open the boot (trunk). Check all the doors and inside the glove box. Look under the seats, and in the magazine holders behind the front seats.

Clear the parcel shelf. Is there anything hanging from the rear-view mirror? Is there anything stuck to the dashboard or the windscreen? Remove everything from your vehicle. Sit in your emptied vehicle. How does it feel? Can you notice the difference? Only put back what is truly necessary.

Step five

Now come back to all those things that you put aside as 'non-garage' things. Ask yourself why each item has been relegated to the outside. Is there really no room in the house? Or is it that you're keeping it just in case? Chances are, if you ever did need it in the future, you wouldn't remember where you'd stored it anyway. If you can't think of an occasion where you will use it in the next six months, consider it obsolete and let it go.

23

Miscellaneous

Now it's time for you to consider all those other spots around the house that we haven't yet dealt with. Don't think for a moment that we're leaving a single corner untouched! You'll need to consider all the spaces that are unique to your home. Whether that's simply a nook under the stairs or a broom cupboard in the hallway, or whether it's a games room or a conservatory, let nothing be forgotten. Think about your patio or garden space. Do you have a basement? Do you have halls or corridors? Do you have an attic or eaves storage? Leave no stone unturned.

You know the drill. Haul it all out. Go through each item, one by one, and ask yourself: Is it useful, is it beautiful, or is it leaving your home?

Letting Go Responsibly

Taking Responsibility for Your Stuff

24

Hopefully you've got full boxes of items that you've realised you don't need, don't want and don't like, and you're ready to let them go. That's great! Now we're ready for the next step – getting rid of them responsibly.

Time, energy and resources have gone into the manufacture and transportation of this stuff, and just because it's no longer any use to you, that doesn't mean it is no use to anybody else. The best outcome for anything you no longer require is finding someone else who does want it and will use it. As responsible citizens, we need to do the best we can to find new homes for the things we no longer want.

If you find the whole process of decluttering stressful, and the idea of trying to rehome everything overwhelming, then do the best you can. We all have different commitments and energy levels. Don't beat yourself up if there is something that you can't find a solution for other than landfill.

However, if you absolutely want to reduce the potential waste and find new homes for all your unwanted items, there is usually a way. It may take longer and it will require more effort on your part, but it will be far more rewarding, you will learn a lot in the process ... and the planet will thank you.

This is not just about rehoming your stuff and reducing your waste. It's about breaking the cycle of consumption. If we want less cluttered homes and lives with less stuff, then decluttering is only one part of the solution. We need to stop accumulating more. We think that decluttering is the hard part, but actually, finding new owners and uses for our stuff can be even harder (depending what it is, of course). Recognising this is what really makes us think twice before bringing new items into our homes.

Dealing with our waste proactively is the best way to understand the issues around our current consumption habits: how easy it is for us to buy things and how complicated it can be to dispose of them responsibly. It can also open our eyes to the alternatives available to us, and change the way we buy and accumulate things in the future.

Over the following chapters we will take a more detailed look at the options for letting go of our stuff responsibly:

○ reuse: how to sell or donate the things we no longer need so that others can reuse or repurpose them

○ repair: how to fix broken things, or find someone who can

○ recycle: how to find the right destination for valuable resources.

Finally, we will really zoom in on what we can learn from the things we send to the landfill.

How to (and why) value the things you own

Having an idea about what something is worth is useful in order to decide the best place for passing it on. The value gives an indication of whether we might try to sell the item: a rare collector's item might be snapped up in an online auction but missed on the shelf in a small-town charity shop (and we can always donate the resulting profit to charity if we feel strongly about donating).

Valuing an item also helps us decide whether donating it is better than recycling, and the kind of platform we might use to find a new owner. The lower the value of an item, the more local the solution needs to be. People will travel further for higher value items. If postage cost exceeds the value, online sites may not be a suitable choice.

An excellent starting point to find out what your items are worth is the online auction website eBay. With over 175 million active users (and growing) looking to buy or sell stuff, there are a lot of transactions happening. You can use eBay to find out exactly what people have sold (or tried to sell) similar items for in the past. As a valuing tool it is free to use, there's no need to sign up and you don't have to sell your stuff there later.

Step one

Go to the eBay homepage and in the search bar in the top centre of the homepage, type in three to five words that describe your item. If you know the brand, size or colour, include this in your search. Press enter, and the page showing current listings will load.

If nothing shows up, widen your search result. Omit some details or choose a more general search term. (If nothing comes up then, try searching the internet to see if any older listings show up. If it's an antique or collector's item, see if there are any specific websites or blogs that explain how these items are valued.)

Step two

You will see a menu bar on the left-hand side of the page. Scrolling down, one of the last options (after 'Delivery options') is 'Show only'. Tick the box 'Completed items'. This will show you every item that was listed over the previous few months. You will get an idea of how many items were listed, which will indicate how popular or rare an item is. You will also see the prices that sellers were asking for, but not what the actual sale price was.

Untick 'Completed items' and tick 'Sold items'. You will now see all of the items that were successfully sold, and the prices they were sold for (the prices will be listed in green). This will give you an idea of the money you can expect to make if you sell your item, and how much you can ask for.

Step three

As you go, take note of the categories and keywords used in the most successful sales listings as well as the price range. If you decide to list your item online, you'll be able to make progress much more quickly.

25

Selling

If you suffer from guilt when it comes to parting with your stuff, or you know that some of your unwanted items are worth good money, selling can be a way of relinquishing some of that guilt or acknowledging that you're happy to let go. It can be the difference between hanging on to something 'just in case' and accepting that you're ready to pass it on, as there's compensation. Maybe the extra income you generate from selling your stuff will be useful, and it's an extra incentive – or even a necessity.

You may be questioning why you'd sell your stuff when you can do the 'right' thing and donate it all to the charity shops. There are reasons why selling can be better than donating.

People who work in charity shops are often volunteers: they aren't experts in calculating the value of stuff. Most would have no idea how valuable your original 1980s action figures are, or how much your designer jacket with the deliberate rips and patches actually cost you. Plus charity shops can't charge big money for items even if they are valuable – that's not their business model and they don't have the market.

So consider selling valuable, unusual or collectable items, or items that are out of season. In fact, whatever items you have, don't rule out selling them, even for a token amount. Shoppers love bargains, and if you sell something directly rather than donating it to a store, you can be sure that there is a person taking your item to a new home.

Remember that people value things they've had to pay for more highly than things that they've gotten for free. In some cases (for example, electronics) if an item is offered for free, people may suspect it's faulty or even stolen. If you feel strongly about donating, you can always sell the items and donate the money to charity afterwards.

There are two main ways to sell your stuff yourself: in person and online. But don't feel limited by these suggestions. There are a number of more specific options for certain categories – for example, consignment stores for clothing (both physical and online) or auction houses for furniture.

Selling in person

Flea markets, car boot sales or swap meets are all options for selling in person. These are organised events with predetermined dates and times (often very early in the morning). You drive there with your stuff, set up a table (despite the name, you sell from a table rather than out of the car boot itself) and the public arrive a little later and shop from the selection. You have to pay to attend. These events are often well established, the organisers will advertise well and you'll have a far bigger market.

If you organise a garage sale at home, you don't have to pay set-up or stall fees, and you get to keep all of the proceeds. You can also choose a time and date that suits you. On the downside, you'll have to advertise yourself, attendance may be low and you'll have strangers rocking up at your house and rummaging through your stuff.

Selling online

Online classifieds sites like Craigslist or Gumtree typically have a national reach, but focus on local trade. They usually work by allowing you to list your items on their website for free (although you may be able to pay for access to premium features), with the buyer contacting you directly via email or phone, picking the item up from your home and paying cash on collection. These sites are usually not well set up for taking payments and posting items, meaning online shoppers buy at their own risk. (There is no real risk to the seller, as the buyer has to transfer payment before the seller ships the item. If an item is lost in transit, there are generally no repercussions for the seller.)

Classifieds can be better for bulky or very heavy items, fragile items and small low-value goods where postage would be more than the item itself. The local approach means no shipping costs, lower carbon footprints and zero packaging. And as buyers can inspect items before they take them away, there's no worrying about returns.

Auction sites like eBay are another online selling option. These sites have far wider (read global) audiences so there is the potential to receive a higher price for your item, and they handle payment processing, meaning you don't have to divulge your

bank details to strangers. While it is usually free to list an item, the site typically takes a cut – around 10 per cent (and if you receive payment electronically via a third-party site like PayPal, expect to pay another 10 per cent for this). Paid features are often also available.

Auction sites can be better for anything small and light enough to be posted, collector's items and clothing. Once the buyer has paid, you simply have to post the item to the address they've provided. For bulky items, customer collections will likely still need to be arranged, and payment can be made then.

Selling online, whether through classifieds or auction sites, isn't foolproof, but these platforms work hard to reduce fraud and keep customers happy. They will have guidelines for transactions and it is important to follow them. Keep track of any correspondence, keep receipts or proof of postage and report any suspicious activity immediately. Most disputes (and honestly, these are very rare) can be solved amicably.

If you'd like to explore the idea of selling online a little further but aren't sure where to start, read on!

Step one

The first decision is which type of site to use. This will depend on what you're selling and where you live. Consider whether postage is a sensible option for your item, and whether a free listing will meet your needs. Once you've decided on a classifieds or auction listing, start looking at individual platforms. Most require users to register if they are buying or selling items, but browsing is usually possible, so get a feel for different sites before you commit.

Step two

Next you need to decide on a price for your item (refer back to pages 152-153 for help with this). Ultimately people will pay what they think something is worth. If you are advertising on a classifieds site and the price is keen, the item will be gone in less than a week (and sometimes in a matter of hours). Conversely, overpriced items won't sell. So if you want something sold quickly, advertise at a low price. If you want more money, be prepared to hold out for longer. Remember – just because you paid a certain amount for something, that doesn't mean it was worth the price.

On an auction site, you will have the choice of a fixed-price listing or an auction. With an auction you choose a starting price and an end date (maybe one, three, five, seven or ten days from the start). Once an auction has started, it needs to run its course: you shouldn't end it before the date you chose. The starting price can be as low as you like … but remember, if only one person bids on your item, that is the price you will have to sell it for, so choose a price you're happy with. Auctions are great if you have a minimum price in mind and no maximum, if you want to try to attract multiple bidders with a low price to push the price higher, or if you're unsure of the actual value.

If you're auctioning your item, think about the end day and time. Buyers sometimes like to watch the end of the auction to put in last-minute bids, so finishing in the early morning or late at night is less practical than finishing in the early evening or on a weekend.

With fixed-price listings, the price you choose is the price that the item will sell for (assuming someone buys it). There is usually an option for the buyer to counter-offer with a lower price. If you're not interested in negotiating, write in the ad description 'price is non-negotiable' and don't allow counter-bids or 'Best Offers'. Fixed-price listings run for longer periods than auctions, and some sites will relist the item automatically if no one has purchased it once the listing has ended.

Fixed-price listings are great if you have a specific price in mind, or if you want the item to be available for someone to buy immediately (rather than waiting for an auction to end). They are also useful during festive periods when people need items within time limits, or when there are multiple similar items already listed (particularly through auctions).

Step three

Choose the most appropriate and relevant category and/or subcategory for your item. Avoid 'Miscellaneous Goods' or 'Other' if you can – they are too vague and people rarely browse these options.

Step four

Now you need to give your ad a title. This is very important. Most classifieds and auction sites have too many items listed to make browsing easy, so most prospective buyers will use the search function. This means you need to make your title as searchable as possible. There will be a maximum character limit so try to use all those characters, and as many descriptive words as possible. If the item is made by a brand, list it (and if the brand also has an acronym, try listing both). Size, material and colour may also be important. You'll need to state what it actually is, and if

there are multiple words that describe your item, try to use all of them. The title is not meant to read well; it's meant to attract interested buyers. For example, 'sofa chair lounge armchair seat settee' will match far more search requests than 'comfy seat'. Also, think about *deliberately* using typos. There may be as many 'draws' listed as there are 'drawers'.

Ask yourself, if you were looking for this online, what would you type in the search bar? Have a look at other listings to see what words have been used in the title – particularly ones with high bids.

If your item is new there are a few acronyms that can be used to save valuable characters:

○ BNWT = Brand New with Tags

○ BNWOT = Brand New without Tags

○ BNIB = Brand New in Box

Step five

To get the best price, you need to be as descriptive as possible in your ad. Some items will allow you to enter a barcode and will pre-fill information. If this applies, check the pre-filled information is correct, and amend if not. There may be prompts that can be filled in; if so, check the box or the labels and fill in as many as possible. This will bring more relevant interested people to your item.

When you write the description, don't assume anything is obvious. Describe the material, colour or functions if necessary. If there's a model number or name, list it. If you know where you purchased it from or the recommended retail price, detail these. If it's a current product you can provide a link to a store for buyers to look at. Some buyers like to know why you're getting rid of it (even if it's as simple as saying it no longer fits or is an unwanted gift – it helps distinguish you from a business seller). Provide measurements and dimensions upfront.

One thing that's really important: be honest. If you've worn it one hundred times but it still looks like new, don't say it *is* new – that's fraud. Say it's worn but it still looks like new. If the colour differs in real life from the photos, say so. If you smoke or have pets, say so, particularly with clothing or soft furnishings. If there are creases or nicks or cracks or scratches, however minor, list them.

For listings with local pick-up, add your location details. If you don't want to put the exact address, put the road name but omit the street number. Give buyers a clear idea of where you are.

Step six

Add *all* the pictures. If you're allowed ten free images, use as many of them as you can! Don't just take one out-of-focus picture of your item. Take the front, the back, the sides, a close-up, labels or branding, and any nicks or damage. Take pictures from different angles, or of different parts. Even if you can find an approriate stock image to include, try to also include an image of your own.

Step seven

Next, if your item will be posted, you need to calculate the costs (even if you want to offer free postage, it's a good idea to know what the costs are). You'll need to know the weight (and possibly the dimensions) of your item, and have access to your local postage prices (you can usually find them online). Most postage services calculate prices in brackets rather than per gram or ounce, so weighing doesn't need to be super accurate. Remember to allow a little extra weight for packaging. You can add a small charge on top of the postage costs to allow for packaging and trips to the post office, but keep it reasonable.

Consider quoting for overseas postage, too. It's not much extra hassle for you if you're going to have to take it to the post office anyway, and offering overseas

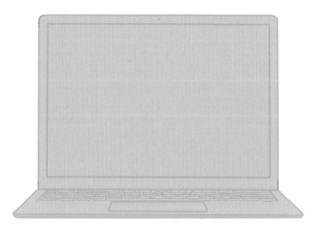

postage makes your item appear in overseas searches. You don't need to quote every country – if you have postage to Europe, the US and Asia/Australasia then you've covered all bases in terms of price points. Don't worry if the postage seems expensive; the buyer is quoted the cost upfront and they will decide if it is affordable. The internal postage cost between countries varies widely and sometimes overseas postage is a cheaper alternative to local postage (crazy as that seems). If you choose not to offer overseas postage, it is helpful to state this in the description. Similarly, if you are happy to post overseas but would rather potential buyers emailed for a quote first, tell them!

Extra considerations for online classifieds

There are a few additional considerations when selling via online classifieds because buyers will come to you to collect the item. Some platforms allow users to communicate directly; others act as an intermediary, meaning your contact details are not shared with the buyer. However, if a buyer is coming to your house to pick up an item, you will need to share your address, and possibly your phone number, with them. If you have a preferred method of contact, say so. Conversely, ask people not to call, or email, or SMS, if you'd rather they contact you a different way.

If you get queries, respond quickly, honestly and cheerfully – and be as helpful and specific as possible. If someone asks, 'Is this still available?', don't just respond 'yes'. Make it easy for people to buy your stuff. Ask when they want to come and look, let them know when you'll be home, give a contact number or even the address. (Also, use your actual name. It's much more personable.)

If you're selling anything big or bulky, let the buyer know about any access restrictions, including stairs, and let them know if they will need someone to help them move the item. If they will need a trolley or other tools, tell them before they arrive. Don't assume they will come prepared!

If an item is electrical, let the buyer plug it in. If it's furniture, let them sit on it. Ask before they arrive if they'd prefer the item neatly packed for them, and if you do this be prepared to unpack the item so they can look at it properly.

Personally, I think it is bad manners to arrive at someone's house and then start negotiating price. My policy is, if buyers try to negotiate at my house, the answer will be no. I'm always completely honest and overly descriptive in my listings, so there won't be any surprises when they arrive. Don't feel pressured to accept less than you want. If they decide not to take the item, someone else will.

Sometimes people arrive with no change. I point them to the nearest ATM/petrol station. If that isn't practical for you, ensure you have change on you. Some people genuinely forget; others might be hoping you'll round down.

The weekend is when most things are bought and sold. Items listed on a Saturday morning will have the most chance of success. You'll need to be home to let people view and collect items, of course, as most people want to collect items at the weekend also.

Safety and security is a personal consideration. I've been using online classifieds for many years without any issues. I've had buyers prefer to do the transaction on the doorstep; others come in (sometimes this is practical and necessary). If you won't feel comfortable with someone collecting items late at night or when you'll be home alone, put preferred hours on your listing. If it's an option, consider asking the buyer to collect from your place of work.

Selling resources

The internet has made it so much easier for people to successfully sell their stuff. New selling sites and platforms pop up all the time; just because an option doesn't appear here, that doesn't mean it isn't worth investigating further. This resource list is a starting point: the most well known and well established of the online selling platforms. Remember, what is popular in one area isn't necessarily popular in your area, and different platforms favour different types of items. See who else is using a platform and what is selling best on each before making your choice, and factor in the different fee structures.

Worldwide

○ **craigslist.org**: an American classified advertisements website started in 1995, which now reaches more than seventy countries. Most features are free, and the site encourages face-to-face transactions, which means no payment processing fees.

○ **ebay.com**: an online auction site that started in 1995. As well as auction-style listings, it also allows 'Buy It Now' purchases and has online classifieds. With thirty-nine country-specific sites and a presence in over 100 countries, eBay has a huge reach of millions of potential buyers.

○ **ebid.net**: an online auction site that began in 1999 and currently operates in twenty-three countries. They charge fees

for casual sellers and offer membership for regular sellers with extra features.

○ **etsy.com**: an online marketplace that allows selling of handmade, vintage (minimum twenty years old) and art-supply goods only. Established in 2005, Etsy charges the seller a listing fee (fixed price) and final sale fee (a percentage of the sale).

○ **facebook.com/marketplace**: Facebook originally launched its marketplace feature in 2007, shut it down in 2014 and relaunched in 2016. It currently operates as a digital marketplace where users can sell or trade items with other people in their local area.

○ **gumtree.com / .com.au**: originally launched in the UK in 2000 as a classified ads and community site, Gumtree is currently the number one classifieds site in the UK, Australia, South Africa and Singapore. Basic listings are free for most people and categories, with premium features available for a fee.

O **letgo.com:** launched in 2015 in the US, Letgo is a free person-to-person classifieds website and app that is optimised for smartphones. Unlike many online classifieds, Letgo lists only goods and not services. Currently the second-fastest growing app in the US, Letgo operates in thirty-five countries and is free to use, with paid features.

UK

O **preloved.co.uk:** a classified advertisements platform started in 1998, currently the second-biggest classifieds website in the UK. Sellers can choose from three membership tiers, and the basic account is free.

O **shpock.com:** an online classifieds app that is image-based rather than text-based, launched in Austria and Germany in 2012 and in the UK in 2014. Free to use with optional charges for premium features, Shpock currently has more than three million users.

US

O **poshmark.com:** a US digital marketplace launched in 2011 that allows people to sell clothing, shoes and accessories, and handles all payment transactions (buying and selling offline is prohibited).

O **webstore.com:** a US classifieds and online auction platform started in 1996 that charges no fees to sellers, instead making money through advertisements and donations.

26

Donating

When we think about donating, we think of the charity shop. Actually, we tend to think of the nearest or most convenient charity shop – but different stores will take different items, so there's no need to limit ourselves to one. Donations don't need to be limited to charity shops, either. We can give items away to community groups, organisations and neighbours – and they'll often take things charity shops might not. You'll be surprised what it's possible to give away to a new home.

Charity shop donations

The most obvious (and easiest) place to donate your unwanted items is the charity shop or thrift store. Remember though – these stores want products that they can resell. That means items that are clean, complete and in good working order. Too many of us are guilty of 'wishcycling' when it comes to making charity-shop donations. We think an item still has some life left and we don't want to throw it out because we feel guilty, so we take it to the charity shop in the hope that they can resell it – even though we know in our hearts that it is extremely unlikely anyone will buy it.

Charity shops get a huge number of donations every day – far more than they can handle. In Australia it's estimated only 15 per cent of all clothes donated to charity shops are resold. We aren't doing charity shops a favour by giving them our stuff: they are doing us a favour by taking it. The best thing we can do is donate only high-quality, well-made and desirable items to charity shops.

Before deciding to donate anything to the charity shop, ask yourself if you genuinely think that someone will walk into the shop and buy the item. If you'd be happy to use it yourself (if you needed it, of course!) or lend it to a friend or family member, then you can donate with a clear conscience. There is no such thing as 'too good for the charity shop'. If items are not up to scratch, don't just throw them away; you will still be able to give them away … just not here.

Other things to consider to give your items the best chance of being resold:

○ Best practice is to call ahead and find out if your local charity shop takes (and needs) the things that you're donating before you drop them off. Some don't have space to take toys or furniture, or may have an overstock or shortage of certain things.

○ Donate direct to the shops rather than donation bins if you can, and try to drop items off within opening hours (or as close as possible) to prevent your donations being damaged.

○ If you do take your items to a donation bin and it is already full, don't just leave your stuff next to it. That's littering. Take it to a different bin or take it home and return at a later date.

○ Try to think seasonally. Stores need to turn over goods fast to make money, and donating all your winter clothes in the height of summer or Christmas-themed tableware in February might mean they don't sell and get sent to landfill, even if they are good quality. If you can, store out-of-season items at home until it is a more appropriate time to donate.

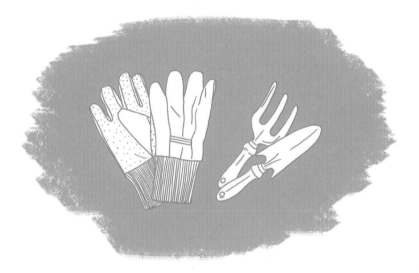

○ In the weeks after the Christmas festive season stores are swamped with donations, and often people aren't buying stuff. Keeping your items in storage for an extra few weeks before donating will increase the likelihood of them selling.

○ Electrical goods can be harder to donate (they need to be tested for electrical safety before reselling, which is not a service all stores can offer) but it is possible! Some charity shops will accept them. Other organisations may accept them to reuse the parts or to repair. Again, check the internet or business listings and if in doubt, call the store.

○ If you have a large number of items or furniture, some charity shops will collect from your home. Check the internet or business listings to find out if anywhere is offering this service.

If in any doubt about anything, call the store and check!

Other places to donate items

Plenty of the stuff we want to declutter isn't really fit for selling or donating to the charity shop: things that are broken (even if they are repairable), items with parts missing, things that have low value, stuff that has been well used, products that have been opened or things that are worn. Not fit for the charity shop doesn't mean only fit for the recycling bin, however. Don't rule anything out – you'd be surprised what other people want!

You might think no one would be interested in old cardboard toilet roll tubes, but actually, there's a thriving trade on eBay among hobbyists. Donating one loo roll tube isn't going to attract much interest, but a whole box of them might be of use to gardeners, or crafters. The same goes for almost anything in large enough amounts. It might be quite hard to donate two glass jars, but if you have three boxes of them, suddenly that's worth the effort for someone who makes jam to come and collect. One magazine might not pique anyone's interest, but an entire back catalogue could. The bottom line is, don't recycle it until you've checked no one wants it!

Online classifieds

Online classified sites like Gumtree and Craigslist are a way to find new homes for unseasonal or unusual items, large amounts of recyclables, incomplete items and broken items (see the selling resources in the previous chapter). You can either list items one by one, or group related items into 'job lots' (for example, grouping kitchen utensils and crockery). Sometimes you need a bit of patience, but there is a new owner out there for everything!

Groups and organisations

Depending on what it is that you're trying to donate, be a little strategic about where to look and who to approach. What kind of person or group might want the items that you no longer want? There will be organisations, groups or clubs who need exactly what you have. Try approaching organisations directly.

O Community gardens – do they need tools, equipment, plants, pots, seeds, soil, even books?

O Craft clubs – if you have anything that hobbyists might be interested in, see if there is an appropriate group near you. Whether it's needlecraft, sewing or knitting, woodwork, modelling or art,

cookery, collecting ... there is a group
out there that will be keen to take your
unwanted stuff off your hands. You just
need to find them!

O Office-based organisations and small
businesses might need office equipment,
furniture, packaging supplies or
stationery.

O Schools and playgroups – do they need
paper and stationery, or office supplies?
Do they need toys or books? Are there
any art or craft projects that they
need supplies for? They may also need
gardening equipment.

O Theatre and amateur dramatics groups
could want furniture, clothing or props
for upcoming productions.

While charity shops accept donations they
can resell, certain charities also accept
donations of goods that they can reuse and
give to people in need: bedding, food and
toiletries, furniture, electronics, and more.
See the donating resources at the end of
this chapter for more information.

Your local community

Another avenue to explore for donating items is with the people in your local community: your neighbours, the people who live on your street, the residents of your suburb. Thanks to social media it is surprisingly easy to get in touch with them. Facebook groups, Google groups and Yahoo groups are popping up allowing us to donate, swap, share and barter with our neighbours.

The Buy Nothing Project is one particularly successful hyper-local community gift-economy initiative. It's only possible to join one Buy Nothing group: the group where you live. The other people in the group are your neighbours, literally. Items can be donated but no money can be exchanged. As people do not have to travel far to collect items, it is a great place to donate low-value items, although high-value items are commonly given away too. From cars and working electronics to broken furniture that needs repairing, from unworn shoes to second-hand packaging, everything is on offer. These local groups are a great way to find out about and connect with other local community groups, and get suggestions for where to offer unwanted items.

Friends and family

Think very carefully before donating items to friends and family. Sometimes we offer things to friends and family as a subconscious way of keeping them close to us: that way, if we ever 'need' them, we can ask to borrow them. Similarly, friends and family can offer to take things that they don't really need or want because they feel bad that we're getting rid of them (maybe they feel that it's a waste of our money, and want to protect us from feeling that we've lost out or made a poor choice). They might have hoarding tendencies of their own – in which case, your extra stuff is definitely not going to help! Remember that when they finally get sick of it, they might try to give it back to you – and you'll be faced with that decluttering decision all over again.

That's not to say that we shouldn't give things to friends and family, but the trick is to figure out what they really need. It's best not to give them all your discards to rummage through – rather, have a casual conversation and find out if there are things they would find useful, and only offer those.

How far you take the quest to donate your unwanted and unneeded stuff is up to you. It will require extra time, and extra effort, and depends totally on your commitment to zero waste, and the energy you have to spare. It doesn't matter if pursuing some of these avenues is too much for you. But if you're someone who hangs on to everything (even broken stuff because you're determined not to waste it), this is your opportunity to find homes for things that you don't need, and let them go.

Charity shop details

Spend some time looking up which charity shops are closest to where you live and work. What are their opening hours? What items do they accept, and what items do they not accept? Make a note of their phone numbers in case you have questions later.

Closest charity shop/s

....

....

Opening hours & location/s

....

....

Phone number/s

....

....

Extra details

....

....

Charity shop checklist

Before packing everything up and taking it to the charity shop, it's worth giving them a call to find out exactly what they will and will not accept. You don't want to make a wasted trip, and they don't want donations of things they can't sell. You can also find out about collection services or alternative solutions for the items they don't accept.

Bedding and blankets	YES / NO	Electrical items	YES / NO
Bicycles	YES / NO	Electronic games	YES / NO
Biscuit and food tins	YES / NO	Fabric	YES / NO
Bottles and jars	YES / NO	Furniture	YES / NO
Bras	YES / NO	Games and toys	YES / NO
Bubble wrap	YES / NO	Garden tools	YES / NO
Buttons	YES / NO	Glasses (reading)	YES / NO
CDs and DVDs	YES / NO	Jewellery	YES / NO
Clothing	YES / NO	Mattresses	YES / NO
Computers	YES / NO	Rags	YES / NO
Crockery	YES / NO	Rugs	YES / NO
Cushions	YES / NO	School uniforms	YES / NO
Cutlery	YES / NO	White goods	YES / NO

Donating resources

Figuring out where to donate our stuff once we are done with it can be harder than the decluttering process itself. Having some clear ideas of the kinds of options available will help you donate your possessions quickly and painlessly. This section deals with two alternative ways to offer items up for reuse: donating to charities or social enterprises that will use the items or pass them on to those in need, and donating to people in our local community who need what we have. (See pages 190-191 for information on donating items to be recycled.)

Charities and social enterprises that use or pass on items

Different charities have different needs, and can be a great way to pass on unwanted items that aren't suitable (or are too 'niche') for charity shops.

○ Animal refuges often accept towels, sheets and other bedding, pet food and possibly other equipment and accessories.

○ Electronics in working order are accepted by some organisations for reuse in underprivileged communities.

○ Food items are accepted all year round by food banks, but at Christmas and other times of year these services may accept toiletries, sanitary items and other non-food items – check with the individual organisation.

○ Opticians often accept used glasses to send to underserviced communities.

○ Refugee centres accept donations of clothing, books, food, furniture, white goods and more.

○ Sports equipment and clothing is accepted by some charities to redistribute to underserviced communities.

○ Women's refuges, homeless centres and hostels accept clothing and blankets and may accept toiletries and sanitary items (be aware that refuges do not usually list their addresses publicly for safety reasons, so you will need to connect with a local charity serving these centres to find out what they will and won't accept).

Lots of these organisations will be community oriented and local. Some national schemes are listed opposite.

Australia

O **fairgame.org.au:** they accept donations of second-hand sports equipment and donate it to remote and underserviced communities around Australia.

O **givenow.com.au:** an online giving platform listing over 4000 organisations, which accept donated items for reuse including bicycles, household goods, clothing, stationery and electronics.

O **refugeecouncil.org.au/donating-goods:** while it does not accept donations itself, the Refugee Council of Australia hosts a database of charities accepting donations (and lists what they will and won't accept) in each state, as well as contact details should you wish to enquire directly with a particular organisation.

O **upliftbras.org:** a registered charity that collects new and second-hand bras, fabric nappies and swimwear and redistributes them wherever they have requests, whether in Australia or overseas.

UK

O **getwellgamers.org.uk:** a registered Scottish charity that accepts donations of video games, video game consoles and accessories, which it passes on to children's hospitals, hospices and other facilities to give sick kids the benefit of entertainment.

O **smallsforall.org:** a registered Scottish charity that accepts donations of new underwear and new or gently used bras in any size (excluding cropped-top or bikini tops) and donates them to women and children in Africa.

US

O **cristina.org:** works to promote technology reuse by connecting non-profit organisations and schools with donors. Their website has a database enabling people with used electronics to find local charities and schools looking for donations of these items.

O **freethegirls.org:** a non-profit organisation working with sex-trafficking survivors in El Salvador, Mozambique and Uganda. They accept donations of new and gently used bras of all sizes and styles, including camisoles, via their drop-off locations or by mail.

O **worldcomputerexchange.org:** a non-profit organisation that accepts donations of computers and other electronics to pass on to those in need. Since 2000, they have donated to more than 3350 schools, youth centres, libraries and universities in forty-eight countries.

Community gifting platforms and networks

Someone, somewhere, wants what you have. Offering up items for free to others in our neighbourhood or community means keeping our stuff out of landfill, stopping new resources being purchased and, best of all: helping someone out. There are plenty of online platforms that make connecting with our neighbours and finding someone to take our stuff easier than ever before.

The best community sharing apps and websites are not the ones with the most beautiful websites and up-to-date technology; they are the ones with the most active users. A beautiful-looking neighbourhood network app where your nearest registered neighbour lives 200 kilometres or 200 miles away is hardly going to be a good tool for donating your unwanted possessions.

The most important questions are:

O How many people in my neighbourhood are using this platform?

O What are they primarily using the platform for? (If selling and donating is our goal, networks that focus on finding lost pets might not be the best choice.)

O Are people active on the platform? (Was the last post in the last hour, day, or month? More recent is always better.)

Worldwide

O **buynothingproject.org**: a hyper-local movement of Buy Nothing groups that operate as Facebook groups, where items can be given away or borrowed (no buying or selling, trades or bartering). People can only join one group: the one where they live, so the other members are literally neighbours, and this makes the whole giving away of unwanted items all the easier.

O **freecycle.org**: a non-profit organisation that coordinates a worldwide network of 'gifting' groups to divert usable goods from landfill. Freecycle currently has a presence in 121 countries.

O **littlefreelibrary.org**: a non-profit organisation that fosters neighbourhood book exchanges around the world with more than 75,000 micro libraries in eighty-eight countries. These libraries can take small numbers of donated books for others to read and enjoy.

O **nextdoor.com / .co.uk**: a private social network for neighbourhoods that launched in the US in 2011 and currently also serves France, Germany, the Netherlands, Spain and the UK. The Nextdoor Australia platform launched in late 2018.

- **olioex.com:** a mobile app for food sharing, currently used in thirty-two countries. Donated food can be raw or cooked, sealed or open, but it must be edible and within its use-by date; the primary guideline is that it is 'good enough for you'.

- **streetbank.com:** described as a movement of people who share with their neighbours, Streetbank (which began in 2010) allows users to choose the size of their neighbourhood (1, 5 or 10 miles) to give stuff away, share things and share skills.

- **transitionnetwork.org:** founded in 2006, this worldwide network of community groups and projects aims to increase self-sufficiency within local communities. An excellent first stop when looking to find out more information about community groups and services in your local area.

- **trashnothing.com:** this website and app work like a custom inbox for various freecycling groups. Emails are diverted here rather than all being directed to your personal email. A useful tool to segregate your decluttering efforts from day-to-day emails.

UK

- **ilovefreegle.org:** founded in 2009, this non-profit organisation offers a free web-based platform to give items away.

Repairing

27

Decluttering usually involves dealing with things that are broken. We let these things languish in our homes, perhaps we buy a replacement, and eventually we decide we no longer need the broken item. But if it was fixed, could it still be useful to someone else? There's a big difference between broken and completely worn out.

The value of a working item is far greater than the value of a broken item, and working items tend to be in greater demand (for obvious reasons). If we repair our items, we can put them back into circulation rather than cutting their useful life short and sending them to landfill.

Consider these options for your broken items:

○ If appropriate for the item in question, contact the company that sold or manufactured the product. Find out if they offer a repair service or sell spare parts. There may be manuals online that detail common problems and how to fix them, or you may be able to troubleshoot error codes online. If you know what part you need, it may be cheaper to buy it from a parts store than directly from the manufacturer.

○ You could try to fix the item yourself. There's a great online resource called iFixit.com empowering people to fix the things they own, with over 44,000 manuals online and even more solutions. Where companies don't make manuals and parts available to independent repairers, iFixit fill the gap. They also sell parts.

○ Alternatively, you could take it to a local repair shop (a business) or a local repair lab or cafe (usually pop-up events rather than permanent establishments, community-led, and for-purpose rather than for-profit). While a repair shop will fix an item for you, a repair cafe might ask that you assist in the repair or even do it yourself under supervision. This is a great way to learn a new skill. The more commonly repaired items are electronics, hardware, white goods, appliances, tools, bicycles, furniture, clothing, shoes and accessories. Whatever the item is, though, it is worth asking the question: Can it be repaired?

Repairing things is the ultimate in letting go responsibly. It's taking ownership, respecting the resources used and the effort that's gone into making the items, and recognising that just because something doesn't work, that doesn't mean end-of-life. Repairing things is the opportunity to make things right and keep useful stuff out of landfill.

I consider a few dollars spent repairing an item of clothing or a pair of shoes before giving it to the charity shop as paying it forward. It's the difference between giving them something they will be able to sell easily and make money from and giving them an item that will most likely end up in landfill and potentially cost them money to dispose of.

When repair is unrealistic

Sometimes the limiting factor for repairing items is the cost. We all have different budgets. If paying to fix something is beyond your means but you still think it worthwhile, consider trying to donate it for someone else to use as parts or to fix. Offer the item, explain what the issue is (and what the fix is, if you know) and you might still find someone to take it off your hands.

This also applies if you think the item could be repaired, but you just don't have the time or energy to follow through with it. Donate it to someone who will.

Repair resources

There are many businesses and skilled tradespeople who can fix our stuff. Mending services for computers and electronics, furniture, clothing and accessories (belts, bags, etc.) are most commonly found.

Use the internet or the local phone directory to seek out professional menders in your area. Alternatively, if you don't have the budget for a professional repair and/or would like to learn some fixing skills yourself, consider a community-led fixing solution. From wholly online information to local workshops, enthusiastic community members are committed to help you keep your stuff out of landfill and give it another life. Some of the bigger networks in community repair are listed opposite, but small, local solutions are too numerous to mention, so be sure to check if anything else is happening in your area.

Online only

O **iFixit.com:** a wiki-based site offering fix-it-yourself manuals plus troubleshooting ideas and more. Anyone can create a repair manual for a device, and anyone can also edit the existing set of manuals to improve them: the project lets those who know how to fix things share this technical knowledge with the rest of the world.

Community-based repair networks

O **repaircafe.org:** with over 1500 locations around the world, repair cafes are free meeting places that are all about repairing things (together). At the repair cafe location, you'll find tools and materials to help you make any repairs you need. Items typically repaired include electrical items, clothing, furniture, crockery and bicycles.

O **therestartproject.org:** based in London but spreading across the globe, the Restart Project run regular Restart Parties where people teach each other how to repair their broken and slow devices: from tablets to toasters and iPhones to headphones.

O **fixitclinic.blogspot.com:** started in California and now active in other states, US-based Fixit Clinic holds pop-up community events where anyone can bring broken items to disassemble and fix.

O **reparatur-initiativen.de:** a German network of repair initiatives coordinated by the Anstiftung Foundation, involving 800 repair cafes across the country. Items being repaired include electrical and mechanical household appliances, electronics, textiles, bicycles, toys and other things.

28

Recycling

Recycling may be presented as a green solution, and it is definitely preferable to landfill, but it uses a lot of resources. Those recyclables still need to be collected, sorted and processed back into 'new' products. That is why recycling is a later consideration in the waste hierarchy, to come only after reusing and repairing. Before consigning anything to the recycling, take the time to consider if there's a better alternative.

If you have any packaging, or any unrepairable, worn-out and broken items then you need to find out where they can be recycled. Recycling can be complicated. Even when you know something is recyclable – and far more items are than you might think – that doesn't necessarily mean your council will collect it, and finding out where to take it can be tricky. Kerbside recycling (if you have it) often collects only a fraction of what can actually be recycled.

If you have a choice between mixed recycling (such as kerbside recycling bins) and recycling that is separated at source (bottle banks for coloured glass), choose the latter. It reduces both the chance of contamination and the handling and sorting required by the recycling company, which increases their margins and makes the commodity more valuable (and more likely to be recycled).

Investigate your local council services

The first step is to check what recycling services your local council offers. If you have a kerbside recycling collection, check exactly what materials can be recycled in this way, and how they need to be packed. Many councils will take paper and cardboard, glass, aluminium cans and foil, steel cans and plastics type 1 and 2 in kerbside recycling.

Councils sometimes offer subsidised or even free services for collection of larger items including furniture, mattresses and white goods. They may also operate transfer stations – these are places to take hazardous chemicals, old paint and larger items, or items not collected kerbside, and are usually open to the public. Check which refuse facilities are located in your area, what they take and what limits and restrictions they have on quantities.

Corporate sustainability programs

Increasingly, corporations are taking more responsibility for their role in creating waste. Try some of these corporate initiatives for your recyclables:

○ Supermarkets, large hardware stores and big retailers will sometimes run recycling programs, usually for products that they sell themselves, including batteries, light bulbs, textiles and water filter cartridges.

○ Electronics manufacturers and retailers sometimes take back electronic equip-ment, printer cartridges and cables. Some take any brand, and others only

their own brand. In some countries this is a legal requirement, but because it is a cost to the company, they are not always keen to advertise it! Check their websites, or call them to ask.

O Increasingly, clothing stores are allowing customers to return own-brand clothing for recycling.

O Soft and noisy plastics (like plastic bags and food packaging) can often be recycled in supermarkets and some-times big box retailers or department stores. Often after the festive season bigger retailers will collect greetings cards for recycling.

Charity shop recycling

Some charity shops will specifically collect textiles for recycling (as opposed to textiles for resale). Usually it is the bigger organisations that do this, so enquire before dropping them off. If you have textiles that are only suitable to be used as rags, keep them separate and label them clearly – it will save someone having to sort through them later.

Recycling resources

To figure out exactly what you can recycle in your area, the first stop is finding your local council website, and reading their information on recycling. If there's anything that's unclear or not mentioned, give them a call to find out more details. (You'll find a checklist at the end of this section.) The following websites should fill in the gaps and help you find alternatives to landfill for those items the council doesn't deal with. Many manufacturers and retailers (too many to list) accept their own products back for recycling so it is also worth checking the brand websites or getting in touch to see if they offer this service.

Worldwide

○ about.hm.com: a global fast fashion brand that accepts old clothes and unwanted textiles (any brand, any condition) at many of their stores worldwide as part of their efforts to improve sustainability.

○ nike.com/help/a/recycle-shoes: an international footwear and sportswear brand that offers a reuse-a-shoe service, accepting any brand of athletic shoe (not sandals, boots or dress shoes) through most of its Nike stores in the US and Europe, and recycling the material for new products.

○ terracycle.com / .co.uk / com.au: a private company that specialises in recycling hard-to-recycle consumer waste (particularly packaging) through a range of free programs sponsored by conscientious companies, and some paid programs where boxes are purchased, filled with the recyclable material and shipped back to TerraCycle (postage is included).

Australia

○ recyclingnearyou.com.au: a website run by Planet Ark (an Australian not-for-profit environmental organisation), which allows anyone to search for what can and can't be recycled in their household recycling services, as well as for drop-off locations to recycle a wide range of items including electronic waste, batteries, printer cartridges, white goods, furniture and more.

○ **National Television and Computer Recycling Scheme (NTCRS):** there are four federal government–approved nationwide recycling services for televisions, computers, printers and computer peripherals:

- mri.com.au/dropzone
- ecyclesolutions.net.au
- epsaewaste.com.au
- techcollect.com.au

○ **paintback.com.au:** an industry-led initiative and not-for-profit organisation diverting unwanted paint and packaging from ending up in landfill or waterways, with collection points nationwide.

UK

○ **recycleforscotland.com:** advice and information on recycling in Scotland, supported by Zero Waste Scotland, funded by the Scottish government and European Regional Development Fund.

○ **recycleforwales.org.uk:** national recycling information for Wales, supported and funded by the Welsh government.

○ **recyclenow.com:** national recycling information for England, supported and funded by government and used by more than 90 per cent of English authorities.

US

○ **earth911.com:** one of North America's most extensive recycling databases, with over 350 materials and 100,000 listings included.

○ **electronicstakeback.com:** a coalition of partner and member organisations promoting responsible recycling of electronics in the US. Their website includes information about 'e-stewards' (responsible recyclers who do not ship hazardous waste overseas for processing and uphold higher standards) and retailers who offer take-back schemes for recycling.

○ **e-stewards.org:** an international team of individuals, institutions, businesses, non-profit organisations, and governmental agencies upholding a safe, ethical and globally responsible standard for e-waste recycling and refurbishment. Their website has a database of certified responsible electronics recyclers.

○ **levistrauss.com/sustainability/planet:** a clothing company that has partnered with I:Collect (a global solutions provider for collection, reuse and recycling of used clothing and shoes) to allow anyone to drop off their no-longer-wanted clothing or shoes (any brand) in collection boxes available at every Levi's store in the US.

Recycle right checklist

All of these items are theoretically recyclable, so find out if they are dealt with by the local council, businesses or other organisations in your area.

Aerosol cans

....

Aluminium

....

Asbestos

....

Batteries

....

Car batteries

....

Chemicals

....

Chemical drums

....

Clothing and textiles

....

Computers and accessories

....

Construction and demolition

....

Corks

....

Electrical appliances

....

e-waste

....

Food scraps

....

Furniture

....

Garden cuttings

....

Recycling

Gas cylinders

· ·

Glass bottles and jars

· ·

Glasses (sight and reading)

· ·

Light bulbs

· ·

Mattresses

· ·

Medicines

· ·

Metals

· ·

Milk and juice cartons

· ·

Mobile phones

· ·

Office paper

· ·

Oil (cooking)

· ·

Oil (used motor)

· ·

Paints

· ·

Paper, cardboard and phone books

· ·

Plastic bottles and containers

· ·

Plastic bags

· ·

Polystyrene

· ·

Printer cartridges

· ·

Steel cans

· ·

Televisions

· ·

Tyres

· ·

White goods

· ·

29

Learning from Landfill

No matter how hard we try to reuse, repurpose, repair and recycle our unwanted items, some things will end up in landfill because they are just too worn, difficult, outdated, expensive or impractical to deal with in any other way. Many items aren't designed with much thought on the part of manufacturers for how they will be disposed of responsibly, and we don't tend to choose products with their end-of-life disposal in mind at the time of purchase.

Ultimately, waste is a design flaw. We can see the items we have no other option but to landfill as an opportunity to learn: about our choices and our habits, and about how to do things differently next time.

Sometimes things are beyond repair. If it's because the item has truly been used up or worn out, or is so old that it is no longer possible to find parts, that is one thing. But if it is beyond repair simply because of bad design, inferior materials and an unwillingness on the manufacturer's part to assist in fixing it (by selling replacement parts, for example) then we can take note of these products, or these brands, and choose not to purchase them in future.

For every brand that's trying to sell stuff as quickly as possible with no intention of the product lasting and no thought about where it might end up, there's another trying to do things a little bit better. There are companies thoughtfully making products that are designed to last, and that encourage repair, reuse or recycling.

We declutter because we want less, and we maintain this by choosing better. By being more conscious of the choices we make, and by selecting products that are suitable for the purpose we want them for, we begin to stop the cycle of accumulation. If we don't buy products that we know will break quickly, and we choose brands that take end-of-life disposal seriously, we keep the things we buy for longer, and stop our purchases becoming a burden – both for us and the environment.

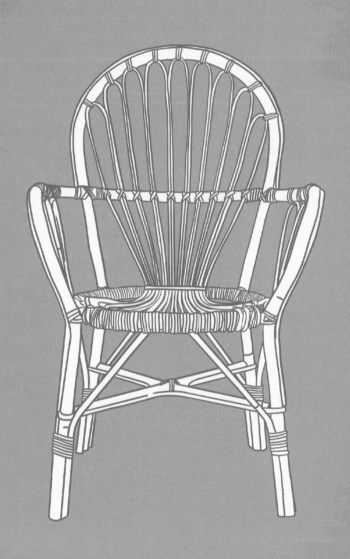

Keeping Clutter at Bay

Tidy Habits

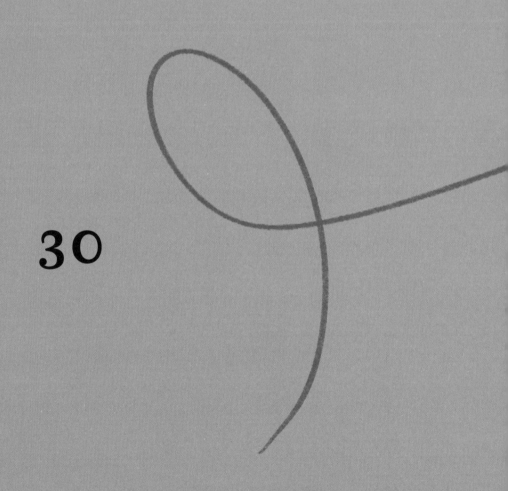

30

If you dream of a tidy and clutter-free home, decluttering is a huge part of the journey; however, it does not guarantee tidiness. Immediately afterwards there will be tidiness, but there is no guarantee that things will stay tidy. If you were a messy person before, decluttering will not transform your home into one that no longer needs tidying. This is an important lesson to learn, and came as somewhat of a shock to me!

Homes need tidying

Houses don't tidy themselves. This took me a long time to figure out. I would often wonder how other people managed to keep their houses clean and tidy. I thought there must be a secret, and if I could just discover it for myself, my home would be miraculously clean. The truth, of course, is there is no secret. They simply do the work. If we want our homes to be clean, we have to be the ones to clean them (or, we hire a cleaner).

And there is no 'once-and-for-all' with cleaning. We can clean until the place is spotless, and everything gleams, but soon enough everything is dirty and dusty and needs to be cleaned again. Rather than save up all the cleaning until it becomes a monstrous job, and resenting how much time it takes, we can accept that there will always be cleaning, and do a little every day. Do the dishes straightaway, and put them away. Do a load of laundry once the basket is full, and put it away. It doesn't seem so much of a chore this way. I'm not perfect, not at all, but when I get lazy and let a few loads of laundry build up or the dishes accumulate in the sink, it's always far more onerous than little and often. Slowly, slowly, the lesson is being learned.

Hopefully as you've decluttered, you've found new homes for things and made more room for what you've chosen to keep. Beyond that, there's no need to overcomplicate things. Complex systems, or boxes with labels and dividers and sub-dividers and headings, or neat stacks of things balanced precariously one on top of the other, all mean extra work and more reason not to put something away properly. One moment of 'I-can't-be-bothered-I'll-do-it-properly-later' shortcut-taking, and the whole system crumbles and the clutter reappears. If you live with other people, making things easy is even more important. The more complicated our systems are, the less likely anyone else will be to follow them.

Simplicity is the key.

Nagging doesn't work

Everyone has a mess threshold: the point at which the mess becomes unbearable and they have to do something about it. If one person in a household grumbles about the mess more than the others, it is likely that they have a lower mess threshold. If we are the ones who have initiated the decluttering or seem to be the only ones who notice the untidiness, it's likely that this is us.

If the other person (or people) in the household can't see the mess or that it requires tidying, then they won't see any urgency in doing the tidying, even if they are asked and agree to help. Which means despite seeming willing to help, they will put it to the back of the list. Of course, if we want it to be tidy, that's when we start to nag, and that's when the resentment begins. If we want to maintain the peace, we have two options. We either need to raise our mess tolerance levels, or accept that *these are our needs*, and we must do the work ourselves.

That's not to say that we need to tidy up after everybody. But rather than resenting other members of the household, or begrudging doing the work, or even refusing to do it ourselves until everyone else joins in, we can accept that this is what *we* want, and tidy up after ourselves. If you want to move everyone else's clutter into a box until they are ready to sort it out, try it. Tidiness breeds tidiness, but new habits take time. Don't give up.

Mindfulness

A tidy home has a lot to do with mind-fulness. Mindfulness can be described as the state of being conscious or aware of something, but it goes deeper that. It's about paying attention in a particular way: on purpose, in the present moment, and without making any judgements. This means seeing the way things are, without believing that they are 'right' or 'wrong' – they just 'are'. It is a state of awareness.

Let me give you an example. If you have a messy home you're probably a little like I can still be: walk in the front door, drop shoes at the doorway, throw coat over a chair, and drop on the sofa after throwing bag on the floor. Keys go in the bag, or on the sofa (probably falling behind the cushions), or remain in a coat pocket, or get left on the benchtop seemingly at random. All the while I am thinking about how my day went (the past), and what I should cook for dinner or my plans for the evening (the future). I look at how messy the house is (making a judgement) and feel annoyed that the dishes hadn't been cleaned before I left (wishing things were different). This is the opposite of mindfulness: thinking about everything except the present moment.

What if, instead of the above, we come home, leave our shoes at the entrance and then walk to the wardrobe and hang our coat and put our bag away (ensuring the keys are in there)? Really, it takes a couple of extra seconds at the time, but it saves us having to go through the whole process of looking for where we've left things and putting them away later, plus it decreases the clutter immediately. What if we put aside our expectations of how we'd like things to be, or how we'd like others to behave, and accept things just as they are in this moment? After all, we can't change the past, and the future hasn't happened yet, so the present is all we actually have. Why get annoyed or frustrated with things that we can't change?

It shouldn't be that hard, should it? Yet if you consider yourself a messy person, it's easy to think that you can't change, or that this won't work for you. Let me tell you, I was a very messy person, and I thought the same. The truth is, being tidy or untidy is not something etched in stone that we have to live with. We can change. Change might not be fast, it might not be easy, and we might not reach the realms of perfection, but it is possible.

Step one

Let go of any negative self-talk ('I'm a messy person') and any negative thoughts about tidying ('tidying is boring'). Telling ourselves that we are messy and dislike tidying reinforces to our subconscious mind that we do not want to tidy! Try changing your tune. If you catch yourself saying that you are messy, reframe it. Tell yourself instead, 'In the past I was messy, but I'm changing.' Or be bolder: 'I used to be messy but now I'm a tidy person.' It doesn't need to be true (yet) – the more you tell yourself this, the more likely it is to become true. Grit your teeth, if you have to! Rather than telling yourself that you dislike tidying, remind yourself, 'I love it when my home is tidy', or even begin the mantra 'I love tidying!' Do this as you tidy and notice how your mood shifts.

Step two

Try not to see tidying as a thankless chore. Instead, try to feel grateful. Feel grateful that you live in your home, and have possessions, and are able to clean. Feel grateful, if you share your home with others, that these people are in your life, and remind yourself of all the things you appreciate about them. It doesn't matter if they aren't the best at tidying up; they have plenty of other (better) attributes that you value. Before you tidy, remind yourself of these things, and know that as you tidy you are creating a better space for yourself and for them to appreciate.

Step three

When you tidy, just tidy. Don't get distracted making plans, or checking your phone, or worrying about other things that you need to do. Practise mindfulness. Notice what you're doing, and how you're feeling. Forget everything else and concentrate only on the task at hand. Relax, and enjoy the moment.

I am not perfect, and no, my home does not look like a magazine cover (not even close). I still get cross at myself for being too tired the night before to do the dishes, or wish that things were different. But I'm slowly becoming more aware, and when I notice these thoughts, I try to let them go.

Cleaning and tidying are two things that will always need doing. We have a choice in the way we approach them. We can either grumble and complain and resist, or we can learn to accept and begin to enjoy the process. Either way, the job gets done, but one brings stress and resentment, and the other brings calmness and clarity. Is there even a contest?

31

The Front Door

Decluttering is hard work (especially if you care about finding good homes for your stuff and avoiding landfill). It can be an emotional rollercoaster, and can bring many of our regrets to the surface. But once the hard work has been done, and we're surrounded by clutter-free spaces, it feels good. There's a calmness and peace to uncluttered spaces that we really can't appreciate until we've experienced it – and the harder the journey has been, the greater this appreciation is.

If we want this calm and peace to remain, we need to remember the lessons we've learned. Decluttering lets us see how much of the stuff we own we truly use and value, and how much is just wasted time, money and resources. It makes us realise that we can live with far less than we thought.

Decluttering shouldn't be an excuse to create space simply to invite more stuff back into our homes! If we want to live free from the stress that too much stuff creates, then we need to think carefully about what we allow into our homes. If we continue to buy needless items, or accept gifts without thinking, then we will continue to accumulate clutter and the benefits of decluttering will be lost.

We are in control of what we let through our front door. Whatever it is, once it enters our home it becomes something else to store and look after. If we don't need it, it will become clutter, taking up physical and mental space until we get round to decluttering it. Rather than letting clutter in and then dealing with it, we need to start thinking about it before it even crosses the threshold.

How do things come into our homes? We buy them. We are given them. Someone else in the household brings them in. We may not have control over the last one, but we are very much in control of the other two.

Before you buy anything, ask the question: Do I need it? Will I use it? Is it worth it? Is it made well and fit for purpose? Can I borrow it rather than buy it, or do without?

When heading out shopping, write a list and stick to it. Avoid browsing or window-shopping, and this is even more important if you're feeling glum, tired, bored or hungry.

Above all, avoid sales and 'bargains'. Remember, you can save 100 per cent of your money if you don't buy anything at all. If it's something that you genuinely need, getting a bargain is great; however, buying things you don't need, just because the price tag tells you that there is a huge discount, means spending money, not saving it.

Beware the Diderot Effect

Have you ever bought something brand new, taken it home and given it pride of place among your other things, marvelled at its shininess … and then realised that your other things look slightly more drab than they did before? Slightly less satisfying, slightly more tired? Maybe it's worth upgrading all of that too?

Before you act on your impulses and head straight back to the shops, be warned. It will only bring tragedy. At least, that's what happened to Denis Diderot. Denis Diderot was an eighteenth-century French writer who was given the gift of a beautiful scarlet dressing-gown. Initially he was very pleased with it. However, he felt his other possessions looked shabby in comparison, and slowly began replacing them with more luxurious ones that matched the splendour of the dressing-gown. His straw chair was replaced with a leather one; a wooden plank bookshelf was replaced with an armoire; some unframed prints were replaced with more expensive artwork.

Not only that, but new items were added: a writing desk, more art, a bronze clock with gold edging and a large mirror over the fireplace. He wanted his home to be as luxurious as he felt while wearing the gown. He even replaced his old maid with a younger, more attractive woman. These new purchases spiralled Diderot into debt, and led him to write the essay 'Regrets on parting with my old dressing-gown, or a warning for those who have more taste than fortune'. He came to regret his new purchases, all the result of the scarlet dressing-gown, and wished he had kept his familiar old robe.

'I was the absolute master of my old robe. I have become the slave of the new one.' Diderot was the first one to write about it, but the experience he describes is actually a recognised social phenomenon – the process of spiralling consumption resulting from dissatisfaction brought about by a new possession, and the subsequent negative environmental, psychological and social impacts. It's called the Diderot Effect.

One way to suppress the Diderot Effect is to buy things second-hand. Pre-owned items don't have same shine as brand-new items, even when they are barely used. They don't stand out in the same way. This means there's less temptation to replace things that don't really need upgrading. Next time you buy something new, you'll probably feel some dissatisfaction with your old things. That's understandable; no doubt the new thing is bright and polished and shiny and packaged splendidly. However, you can be mindful of these feelings without acting on them. Let the feelings pass. There's no need to rush out to the shops to replace everything else. Shiny new things fade with time. Unpaid credit card bills don't.

Unplug

It's estimated that we are bombarded with up to 5000 adverts daily. Some research suggests we will only take notice of around 500 of those adverts a day, claiming that our senses can't cope with any more – but whether it's 500 or 5000, that is still a lot. Especially when most of these adverts have one thing in common: they are designed to make us want to buy more stuff.

Adverts work mostly by trying to make us believe that our lives will be better if we buy the product in question. They usually feature happy, attractive people who appear to be relaxed, loved and successful; these people live in beautiful homes, and have beautiful friends and family members. In this way advertisers tell us that their product is linked to affluence and success ... and happiness.

Countless studies have shown that the more people focus on materialistic values like wealth, image and status, and consider possessions to be important to them, the less happy they are. In fact, people who prioritise these values are more likely to be anxious and depressed – and these psychological problems have been demonstrated to go up as materialistic values go up. Whereas intrinsic values like spending time in nature, connecting with people and helping others, studies show, are what truly make us happy.

Some adverts focus on wealth and success to sell their products, whereas others will try to tap in to intrinsic values by showing families or friends coming together, or people enjoying nature, but the message is the same for both: you must buy the product to be happy.

When we think about our favourite memory, we think about people, places and experiences. No one remembers their best day of TV. We know that these shared experiences and connections are what we treasure, and what make us happy. Yet every time we see an advert we are told a different story: that we need to consume and buy more stuff to find happiness. If we are told that message 5000 or even just 500 times a day, it's no wonder that it begins to stick.

If we want to consume less, we need to step off the consumer treadmill, and the best way to do this is to stop exposing ourselves to adverts. It is difficult to remove adverts entirely, but there is plenty that we can do.

○ Put a 'no junk mail' or 'no advertising material accepted' sticker on your letterbox.

○ Download an ad blocker for your mobile, your tablet, your laptop and/ or your desktop. This will stop those banner ads and sidebar ads appearing on your screen.

○ If you don't use an ad blocker, use private browsing when shopping online: this prevents targeted ads following you around later showing you products.

○ Unsubscribe from retailer newsletters, or anything you receive via email that is spammy and filled with adverts. Don't just delete them. Take the next step.

○ Consider choosing premium versions of apps that come without advertising.

○ Choose to listen to an ad-free radio station or music streaming service.

○ When you walk, cycle or drive, see if you can find a route that avoids billboards or bus stops with adverts plastered on them.

○ Get rid of your TV, or if you can't bear the thought, save your programs for later so you can skip the adverts, or turn the sound down when the adverts are on.

○ If getting rid of your TV seems too extreme, try unplugging it and removing it from your living room for a single week. As well as reducing your exposure to adverts, you'll be amazed at how much more free time you have.

When we're exposed to adverts every day, we don't really notice the impact they have on us. That doesn't mean that they aren't having an impact. We know that more stuff and endless consumption isn't going to make us happy. Don't let the adverts tell you otherwise.

The front door is your last line of defence before stuff enters your home. Work hard to protect it from an influx of new clutter.

Another word on gifts

We're given things all the time. From receipts, flyers, samples and free gifts to thank-you notes, birthday presents and hand-me-downs; these items flow into our homes. Often we take them without thinking, but if we want to keep our homes clutter-free, we need to be more mindful.

Rather than just accepting a receipt, flyer or business card, ask yourself if you really need it. Can you just put the details in your phone or take a quick picture instead? Do you really need to try the sample or take the free promo bag (full of items you probably won't use)? If you do pick these things up without thinking, pop them in the recycling bin, if appropriate, before you get into your home. That way they haven't entered your home and you won't need to deal with them later on.

Gifts are different. Handing a gift back probably won't win you any friends (although it will guarantee you won't receive gifts in the future). To avoid waste and unnecessary clutter, think ahead. If you have a birthday coming up, ask friends and family not to buy you gifts. If you know they will struggle with this idea, suggest an activity or experience you can do together. Writing gift lists for yourself can mean asking for things that you don't really need, and family and friends will often interpret your requests differently to how you intended, meaning you might not get what you wish for anyway. It also encourages unnecessary consumption. Ask yourself if there is anything you genuinely need and don't browse websites or catalogues for 'inspiration'.

If you do receive a gift, accept it graciously. If it's not something you love or something you need, let it go straightaway. Don't dwell on

it – act before the guilt or negative feelings set in. Using it once as a token gesture is likely to only make you feel worse, and new unused products will be more appealing to someone else if you donate or sell them. The meaning of a gift is in the giving, not the keeping of the item in perpetuity. Remember, you don't need to tell the giver what you did with their gift. If they ask, and you don't want to hurt their feelings, say you lent it to someone, or took it to work, or whatever you think of. It's unlikely they will ask again. Do you remember all the gifts you've given over the years? Have you ever asked what became of them?

Gifts can also be unwanted items that other people own and no longer want, and offer to us. They could feel guilty about the waste (money or resources), and so pass them our way. Particularly if we have a reputation as someone who hates waste or likes 'things', we can become a magnet for this stuff! But it's not our job to save other people's stuff from landfill, or alleviate their guilt. However hard it can be, we can say no, and let them take responsibility for their choices. If you are willing to drop it off to the charity shop, sell it or make good use of it, by all means accept it – but take action as soon as you can. If you don't have the time or energy to deal with it, don't feel guilty about saying no. We can only do so much.

Choose Better

32

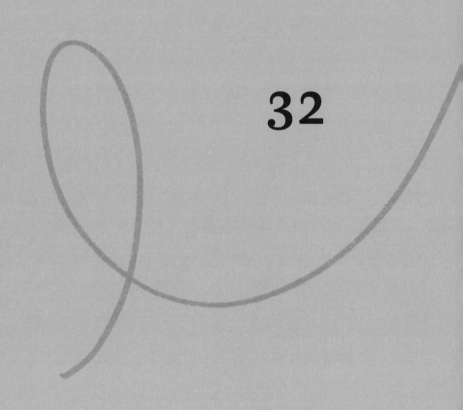

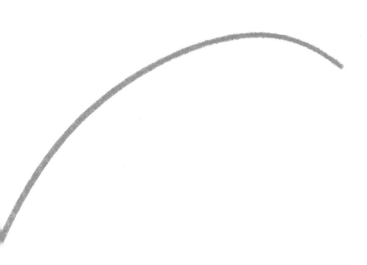

Often when we declutter, we can get stuck in the past. When we feel guilty or regretful, we mistake keeping things that we don't need or don't like as the solution to this guilt. It doesn't work. Letting go means accepting that life didn't quite go the way we intended, and yes, maybe we made poor choices. It's happened to all of us, believe me! None of that matters now; it's all in the past and behind us. Remember that. Heading into the future, we can feel confident that this time, we can choose better.

Choosing better doesn't guarantee we won't make mistakes in the future. Life has a habit of unfolding in ways we don't expect. Hopefully we'll make fewer mistakes, and we won't repeat any of our earlier ones, at least! And when we do make mistakes, that doesn't matter either: that's how we learn, after all. Choosing better means taking the lessons we've learned along the journey and using them to make better decisions.

The things you've decluttered will tell you a lot about yourself and the choices you made in the past. Look for patterns. Ask yourself why you chose to buy these things, or why you held on to them for so long. Was your shopping driven by how you were feeling at the time? Did you tie your identity (or how you wanted to be perceived by others) into the things you bought? Understanding your previous decisions can help stop you repeating the same patterns again.

Before buying something, ask yourself if you really need it. Can you borrow it? Can you make do without? Remember, liking something doesn't have to be a reason to buy it. There will always be beautiful items, and we can appreciate them without owning them. If you don't need them, don't be tempted. Appreciate them from afar. When you decide to buy an item or accept something into your home, look closely at how it's made and what it's made of. Is it built to last? Will it be easy to repair, or

to recycle? Think about the end of its life before you make the choice to take it home with you.

Also think about whether you need to buy it new. As well as saving resources, second-hand items often cost less than new ones. If you change your mind later, you can resell and should be able to recoup most of your outlay, which helps reduce the guilt we feel when we let go of stuff. (Although if there's any doubt that you'll actually use it when you buy it, you probably shouldn't be buying it at all!) Plus, by buying second-hand you'll probably be helping someone else declutter, and you're reducing the amount of 'stuff' in the world. Let's face it, there's enough 'stuff' already.

Consider the places you make your purchases, too. Are they the kinds of stores you're happy to support? Are they responsible retailers that contribute positively to society and the environment? Do they sell quality products that last? Do they support mindful consumption, or do they encourage reckless spending and unnecessary upgrades? When we buy less, we can choose to spend better. We can vote with our wallets for the kinds of businesses we want to see supported. This is your chance to start afresh – to begin a new chapter of your life, or a new journey. This is your chance to focus on what you truly believe to be important.

Remember at the start of this book, when you really drilled down into what it was that you valued in life? How you wanted to spend your time, and your money, and your energy? Now is your chance to take those thoughts and those dreams, and make them your reality. My hope is that you will take the experiences, insights and lessons that this journey has provided, and use them to choose better.

About the Author

Lindsay Miles is a passionate zero-waste and plastic-free living spokesperson and educator who helps people to find more meaningful lives with less waste and less stuff. She has been sharing ideas and strategies on her popular website, Treading My Own Path, since 2013, and has been featured by the ABC and BBC, Channel 9, *The Guardian*, Seven West Media, *The Sunday Times*, TreeHugger, TEDx and more. She gives talks and workshops to encourage others to embrace change, reconnect with their values and make a positive impact on the world. Lindsay lives in Perth, Western Australia.

Acknowledgements

I'd like to acknowledge the lovely team at Hardie Grant for helping me to turn my thoughts into an actual book and for all their enthusiasm and support along the way. Particular thanks to Arwen, who championed my ideas from the beginning, and a huge thank you to Erin, who introduced me to Arwen and in doing so got the whole project started.

To everyone who has ever read or listened to my words, thank you. It encourages me to know that so many of you are embracing a life with less waste and less stuff, and I love the community we have created. My journey has been so enriched for having you join me along the way.

Glen, thank you for believing in me even before I wrote my first words, for reading and re-reading my drafts, being my sounding board, showing enthusiasm for my ideas, and for reassuring me when things got a bit hard. To Helmuth, Eugenie and Rosie: thank you from the bottom of my heart. Your support has meant everything to me, and I'm grateful every day. I truly couldn't have written this book without you.

Index

Published in 2019 by Hardie Grant Books,
an imprint of Hardie Grant Publishing

Hardie Grant Books (Melbourne)
Building 1, 658 Church Street
Richmond, Victoria 3121

Hardie Grant Books (London)
5th & 6th Floors
52–54 Southwark Street
London SE1 1UN

hardiegrantbooks.com

All rights reserved. No part of this publication may be reproduced,
stored in a retrieval system or transmitted in any form by any means,
electronic, mechanical, photocopying, recording or otherwise, without
the prior written permission of the publishers and copyright holders.

The moral rights of the author have been asserted.

Copyright text © Lindsay Miles 2019
Copyright illustrations © Ngaio Parr 2019
Copyright design © Hardie Grant Publishing 2019

 A catalogue record for this
book is available from the
National Library of Australia

Less Stuff
ISBN 978 1 74379 544 6

10 9 8 7 6 5 4 3 2 1

Publisher: Arwen Summers
Project Editor: Emily Hart
Editor: Sonja Heijn
Design Manager: Jessica Lowe
Designer and Illustrator: Ngaio Parr
Production Manager: Todd Rechner

Colour reproduction by Splitting Image Colour Studio
Printed in China by Leo Paper Product LTD

This book was printed on paper certified by the FSC® and other controlled material